AUTOMOTIVE ALTERNATORS

by

AEA Service Division
Automotive Service Industry Association

Howard W. Sams & Co., Inc.
4300 WEST 62ND ST. INDIANAPOLIS, INDIANA 46268 USA

FIRST EDITION
FIRST PRINTING—1977

International Standard Book Number: 0-672-21467-9
Library of Congress Catalog Card Number: 77-83683

Printed in the United States of America.

Preface

In order to efficiently service modern automotive charging systems, the technician should have a working knowledge of automotive alternators (ac generators) and regulators. In addition, he should be familiar with specific troubleshooting procedures for the various makes of alternators. The purpose of this book is to provide the automotive technician with a thorough understanding of the alternators and regulators now in use.

This book begins with a discussion of the requirements of automotive charging systems and the essential differences between generators and alternators. The principles that make an alternator work, including the fundamental properties of electricity and magnetism, are discussed in detail. The operation of automotive alternators, both electromechanical and solid-state, is also thoroughly covered in this book. Various alternator troubleshooting procedures are described, including on-the-vehicle tests and bench tests. The last four chapters of the book give specific troubleshooting procedures for charging systems used by General Motors, Chrysler, Ford, and American Motors.

If you are just entering the automotive service field, this book will prove very informative. The experienced automotive service mechanic will also find this book a useful reference source when servicing charging systems.

Grateful acknowledgment is extended to the following manufacturers for their contribution of illustrations and data.

American Motors Corp.
Chrysler Corp.
Ford Motor Co.
General Motors Corp., AC-Delco Div.
Motorola, Inc.
Kal-Equip Co.
Marquette/Applied Power Inc.
Owatonna Tool Co.
Sun Electric Corp.

Contents

CHAPTER 7

CHAPTER 8

CHAPTER 9

CHAPTER 1

Introduction

In the beginning, the automobile was almost strictly a mechanical contrivance. Electrical devices were confined solely to the ignition system, some of which were powered from a bank of dry cells. When these dry cells were used up, the engine stopped running until new ones were installed. The rechargeable storage battery was yet to be adapted to the newfangled "horseless carriage." Some of the early vehicles used magneto ignition systems which did not depend on any outside power source such as dry cells. The magneto contained its own generator to produce the current needed for ignition.

Lighting, for those daring enough to venture out after dark, was provided by acetylene lamps. And starting those primitive and often balky engines was frequently a contest of muscle versus machine. Early autos were truly for robust and adventurous souls.

The picture changed about 1914 when a practical electric starter motor was developed. This, of course, required a high-capacity storage battery for cranking power, which in turn, necessitated another system to keep it charged. Thus, the automotive charging system began its long period of evolution.

Many schemes were devised to handle these new electrical requirements, most of which now are only of historical interest. Some auto manufacturers combined the starter and generator into one unit which could be attached to the engine. Other manufacturers actually built the starter and generator into the flywheel so that it became an integral part of the engine. Imagine servicing a system like that! Gradually, though, the system that survived was the one we now take for granted—a separate starter system and a separate charging system.

The charging system itself has gone through its own developmental process, first with rudimentary generators, then with more sophisticated generator-regulator circuits, and finally to our present-day alternator system. It is the alternator system that we will concern ourselves with in this book. But to gain a better understanding of alternators, it will be helpful to make a brief comparison between the earlier generator systems and the modern alternator system.

Someone once said that "an alternator is simply a generator turned inside out." You will see that there is some truth to this as we make our comparison. Actually, the difference between the two is primarily mechanical; electrically, both work on the same principles. Although we will discuss the electrical operation later, we will mention one very important electrical characteristic that applies equally to generators and alternators.

In order to produce or generate an electrical current, which, of course, is the main function of a generator or alternator, three things are necessary. First, there must be a magnetic field. Second, there must be an electrical conductor (winding) to carry the generated current. And third, there must be relative motion between the magnetic field and the conductor. Combining these three requirements in a practical device produces a generator or an alternator. The difference between the two is simply the manner in which these requirements are met.

Let's assume that Fig. 1-1 represents a basic generator. For clarity, we have stripped the generator to its barest essentials. The *magnetic field*, the first requirement, is provided by an electromagnet (not shown) wrapped around two soft-iron pole pieces. These pole pieces fasten to the frame of the generator and therefore remain stationary. The current carrying *conductor* or winding, the second requirement, is wrapped in

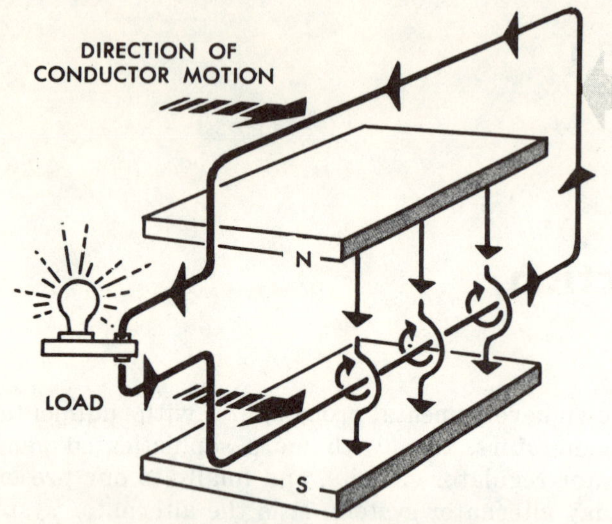

Fig. 1-1. The essential elements needed to generate an electrical current.

loops around an armature (not shown). For simplicity, only one loop is shown. The armature in an actual generator would be made to rotate, thus meeting the third requirement of relative *motion*. For the moment, we won't worry about how the conductors in the armature are connected to any outside load such as a battery.

This simple device will actually generate a current when the armature is made to rotate between the pole pieces. Unfortunately, the current that will be generated is alternating; that is, the current will change direction, first flowing one way then the other as the armature makes one complete revolution. Alternating current (ac) may be fine for household use, but is useless for automotive applications because a battery can be charged only with direct current (dc).

To remedy this situation, generators contain a commutator/brush system which is shown in Fig. 1-2. The commutator/brush system serves two functions. First, it provides a means of connecting the conductors in the rotating armature to an outside circuit and, second, it serves as an automatic reversing switch to convert the ac current generated in the armature windings to the necessary dc current for charging the battery. Each armature winding terminates at two commutator bars as shown in Fig. 1-2. The number of commutator bars depends on the number of armature windings. The current generated in the armature windings is picked up by the carbon brushes and fed to the various electrical circuits. It is not necessary, for our purposes, to explain the details of how the commutator accomplishes its mechanical *rectification* (conversion of ac to dc). The important thing to remember, though, is that the current generated in the armature windings initially is ac.

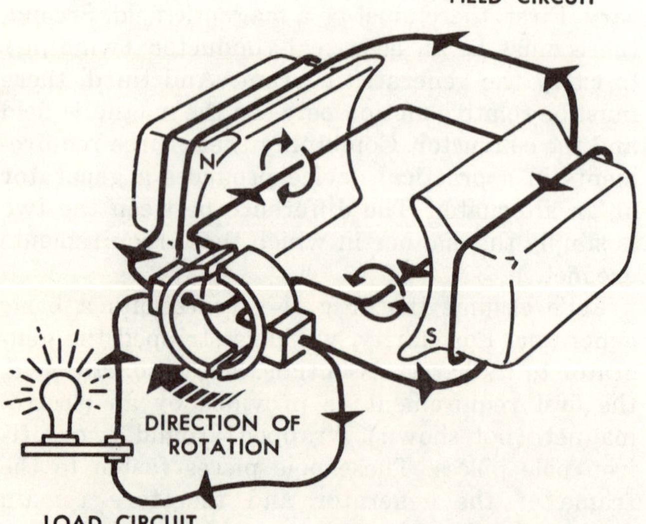

Fig. 1-2. The basic components of a dc generator.

We have now seen, in a rather basic and simplified form, how a generator is able to produce a dc current for charging a battery or operating other electrical devices. Now we will make a similar study of modern alternators, pointing out their similarity to generators. As we do this, keep in mind the three requirements needed to generate a current: (1) a magnetic field, (2) a current-carrying conductor or winding, and (3) motion.

Fig. 1-3 shows the basic components of an alternator. The current carrying conductors are wound on a *stator* and, as the name implies, remain stationary. The electromagnet that produces the magnetic field is wound on a *rotor,* which is connected to a pulley and rotated by the engine. This provided the necessary motion between the magnetic field and the stator conductors. Current is generated in the stator windings just as it was in the generator armature. The only difference, of course, is that the current producing windings of the alternator are stationary; it is the revolving magnetic field of the rotor that provides the relative motion. So, fundamentally speaking, an alternator generates current in the same manner as a generator.

But, just as in a generator, the current being generated in the stator windings of an alternator is ac. To be useful for automotive purposes, the current must be converted or rectified to dc. Unlike the generator which rectifies its output mechanically with the commutator brush system, the alternator accomplishes the same thing with a system of *diodes.* These are solid-state semiconductor devices that allow current to flow in one direction but not the other. We will cover these diodes in more detail in a later chapter.

Notice in Fig. 1-3 that the current needed to excite (energize) the electromagnet in the rotor is fed in through a slip-ring brush system.

Let's summarize the similarities and differences between generators and alternators:

1. The current producing windings are stationary in an alternator but rotating in a generator.
2. The magnetic field revolves in an alternator but is stationary in a generator.
3. The rectification from ac to dc is accomplished by a diode system in an alternator and by a commutator brush system in a generator.

Perhaps now the statement made earlier that "an alternator is a generator turned inside out" makes a little more sense. But you are probably wondering, since both systems do the same job, if there must be an advantage to the alternator system. Otherwise why would its use be so widespread? Actually, there are many advantages of the alternator over the generator system.

Perhaps one of the more important advantages, in view of all the accessories being added to the engine, is the compactness of the alternator. Also, high-current outputs—some presently in the 100-ampere range—can be obtained without materially increasing the size of the alternator. Such outputs are becoming more common with the ever-increasing electrical loads found in today's cars.

Another factor making such high outputs possible is the fact that the output current does not have to pass through a commutator brush system as it does in a generator. Brush life in a generator is affected by the amount of current that they must handle; there is always a certain amount of arcing that takes place as the brushes slide from one commutator bar to another. Dressing the commutator and replacing the brushes were fairly common servicing operations on generator-equipped vehicles.

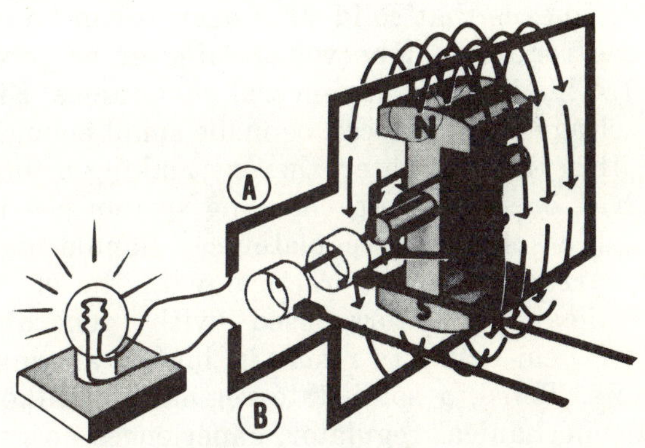

Fig. 1-3. The basic components of an ac generator or alternator.

Although alternators also have brushes (some special alternators are brushless), their longevity is exceptionally good. This is because the amount of current they must handle is exceedingly low—only the few amperes needed to energize the field or rotor winding—and also because they ride on smooth, continuous slip rings. Naturally, even alternator brushes wear down, but not nearly as rapidly as generator brushes.

Another advantage, particularly from a cost and maintenance standpoint, is that it is very easy to *regulate* an alternator. We will be discussing regulation in some detail in Chapter 3, but for now we will say that an alternator requires only voltage regulation. In other words, a small, single-function control unit can provide all the regulation needed for an alternator. A generator, on the other hand, normally requires three control units. In addition to voltage control, a generator also needs current control. Without some form of current control, a generator can produce enough current to damage itself. (Note: Some early generators used a "third" brush to achieve current limitation, thus eliminating the need for a separate current control.) The third control is a cutout relay which opens the circuit between the battery and generator and prevents the battery from discharging back through the generator when the engine is stopped.

The alternator, because of its inherent characteristics, requires neither a current control nor a cutout relay. The maximum output current is limited by alternator design. Because the rectifying diodes normally block current in the reverse direction, the battery cannot discharge through the alternator when the engine stops.

The fact that an alternator requires only voltage control means that solid-state devices can be used for the regulator (the voltage limiter or control unit). This in itself has several advantages. First, the voltage regulator can be made small enough to fit within the alternator, thereby making a totally integral, or single-unit, charging system possible. Second, a solid-state regulator can handle higher field currents than is practical with the electromechanical regulators used with generators. Higher field currents result in higher alternator outputs. Third, a solid-state regulator, unlike an electromechanical regulator, experiences no gradual wear or deterioration. In theory, it can last indefinitely.

However, theory is still theory and, despite the numerous advantages of alternators over generators, alternator systems are not completely trouble-free. While alternators may not experience the same problems that beset generator systems and perhaps do not give trouble quite as often, they still have their own particular problems. Rectifier diodes do break down, solid-state regulators do fail, electrical windings still short out, and connections corrode and open. The task of the service technician is to know whether the system is functioning normally or not and, when trouble is indicated, be able to determine just where it is located.

This, then, is the purpose of this book. The first five chapters will cover the theory and operation of alternator systems in general. Particular attention will be given to testing and troubleshooting these systems, both on-the-vehicle and on the bench. The remaining chapters will deal with specific servicing procedures as outlined by the various manufacturers of alternator systems. Although there is naturally a certain amount of similarity among the various makes and their servicing procedures, there are also specific differences. So be sure to follow the recommended testing and servicing procedures as spelled out by the respective manufacturers.

CHAPTER 2

How Alternators Work

In the first chapter, we briefly described the essential differences between generators and alternators. In this chapter, we will be taking a much closer look at principles that make an alternator work; particularly at those principles that will aid us in testing and troubleshooting the charging system. By having a fuller understanding of how an alternator works, you will be in a better position to know what is wrong when an alternator fails.

However, before we delve into the workings of the alternator and the method by which it produces current, we should first review some of the fundamental properties of electricity and magnetism. After all, an alternator (or a generator, for that matter) is basically an electromechanical device that relies on magnetic properties for its operation.

MAGNETISM

Just what is magnetism? Strangely enough, scientists cannot give us a precise answer. We really don't know what creates this strange force or even why it exists at all. The dictionary defines it as ". . . that property possessed by various bodies, such as iron or steel, of attracting or repelling similar substances according to certain physical laws." Although we cannot say exactly what magnetism is, we do know how it behaves, how to produce it, and how to harness its strange powers for useful purposes. Interestingly enough, most of what we know about magnetism has been discovered only in the past 150 years.

However, magnetism, or rather magnetic effects, were known in ancient times. In fact, it is believed that the word "magnetism" is derived from a particular form of iron ore, known as *lodestone,* that originally was found near the ancient city of Magnesia. A lodestone is a natural magnet that, as early experimenters discovered, had the power to attract pieces of iron (Fig. 2-1). The lodestone remained merely a scientific curiosity until about the 11th or 12th century when it was discovered that an iron needle, made magnetic by rubbing against a lodestone, pointed toward the earth's north pole. Hence, the magnetic compass was invented.

From this it was learned that a magnet, either natural or artificial, had two *poles*—a north pole and a south pole. The end of a magnetized needle that pointed to the earth's north pole was, logically enough, called the *north pole* of the needle. Conversely, the other end was named the *south pole.* This phenomenon also led to the conclusion that the earth itself was a giant magnet, because it was known that unlike poles attracted each other whereas like poles repelled (Fig. 2-2). This behavior of a magnet illustrates an unusual and little-known fact: The earth's geographical north pole must be, in reality, a *south* magnetic pole. If it were not, the north pole of the compass needle

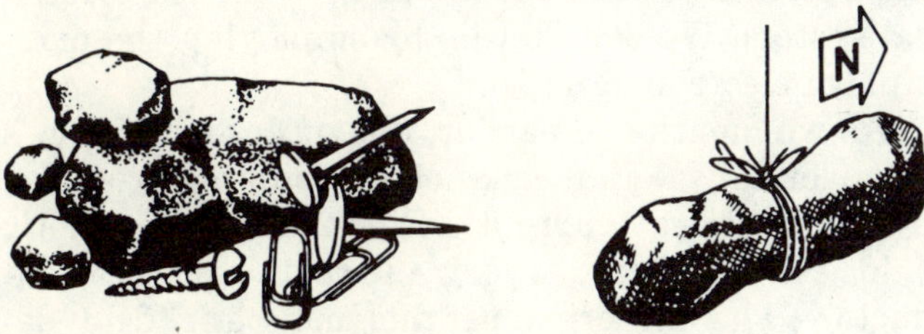

Fig. 2-1. Lodestone, or natural magnet, attracts pieces of iron.

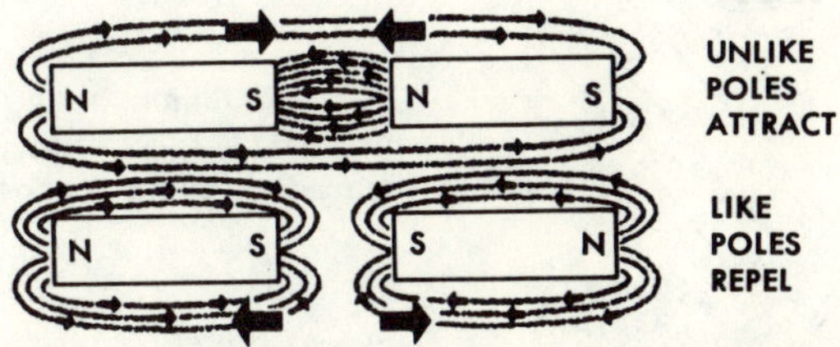

Fig. 2-2. Like magnets repel and unlike magnets attract.

would not point toward the earth's geographical north pole.

This was about all that was known about magnetism until the year 1819 when it was discovered that there is a relationship between electricity and magnetism. This was demonstrated by placing a compass near a wire, as shown in Fig. 2-3, and then passing a current through that wire. The compass needle deflected, proving that a magnetic field existed around a wire carrying an electrical current. When the current ceased to flow, the compass needle returned to its normal position. After this discovery, major strides were made in magnetic theory and its practical application, principally by Joseph Henry, a great American scientist.

One of Henry's most notable discoveries was that not only could magnetism be produced electrically, but that electricity could be produced magnetically. It is this unique characteristic that has made possible our present-day utilization of electricity; without it, virtually all the electrical products we know and use today would be nonexistent. And the few electrical devices that could exist without employing magnetism in one way or another—a battery-operated light, for example—would simply be expensive novelties or merely laboratory curiosities.

Now, let's take a closer look at the more important principles of magnetism and electromagnetism to help us better understand the way an alternator works. First, what is the difference between a magnetized and an unmagnetized piece of iron or other magnetic material? Again, we really don't know that much about magnetism, but the generally accepted theory states that a magnetized piece of material consists of a great number of small, magnetized particles all aligned in the same direction. This is shown in Fig. 2-4. All the north poles point in one direction and the south poles point in the other direction. When the material is unmagnetized, the individual magnetic particles form a random pattern with no predominate magnetic polarity.

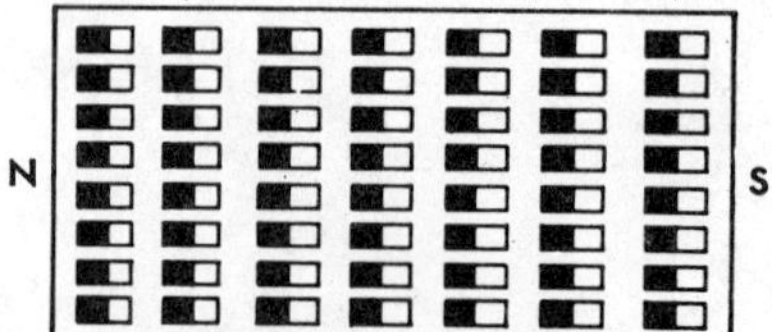

Fig. 2-4. Alignment of magnetic particles in unmagnetized and magnetized iron.

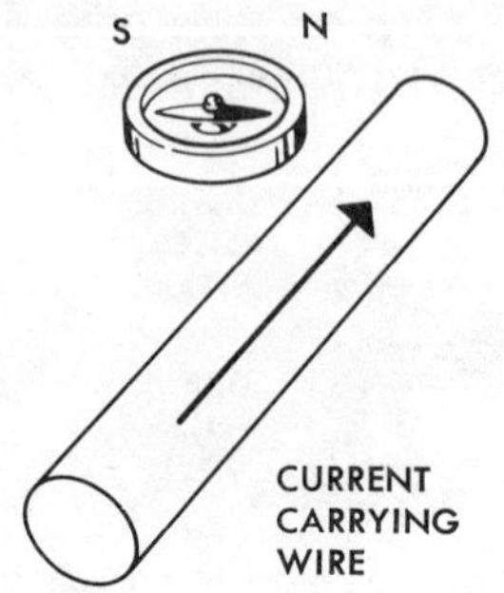

Fig. 2-3. Demonstrating the magnetic field surrounding a current-carrying conductor.

Whether or not this is the way magnetism really works is not really important for our purposes. The important point is that we can magnetize and demagnetize iron at will. It is due to this principle that we are able to generate and *regulate* the current in an alternator. If we were unable to control the magnetism or magnetic field in an alternator, the current we generate would be of little use to us. We will cover the regulation phase of alternators a little later. For now, let's look at the way in which magnetism is produced electrically.

ELECTROMAGNETISM

A permanent magnet, such as a lodestone or the familiar "horseshoe" magnet, has a certain magnetic strength that is fixed and cannot be varied. For many applications, such as electrical meters or loudspeakers, this constant magnetic flux is essential. But in the case of an alternator, it simply will not do the job. We must be able to turn the magnetic flux on and off to meet the widely varying operating requirements of the vehicle's electrical system. We can do this by employing the principle of electromagnetism.

As we mentioned earlier, one of Joseph Henry's discoveries was that magnetism could be produced by an electrical current (Fig. 2-3). A magnetic field exists around every current-carrying conductor. The direction of this magnetic field depends on the direction of the current flowing in the conductor as shown in Fig. 2-5.

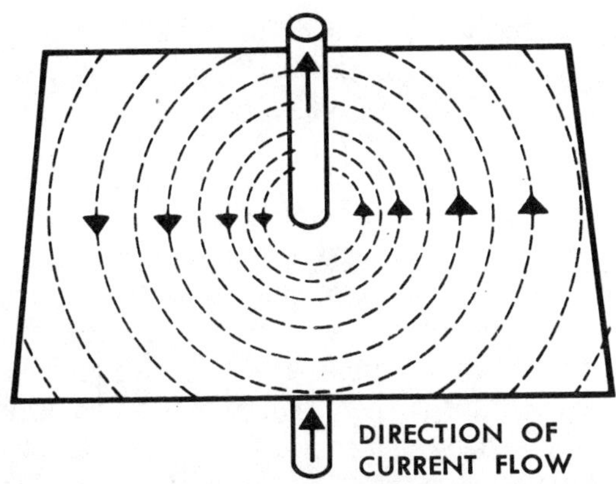

Fig. 2-5. The direction of the magnetic field around a current-carrying conductor.

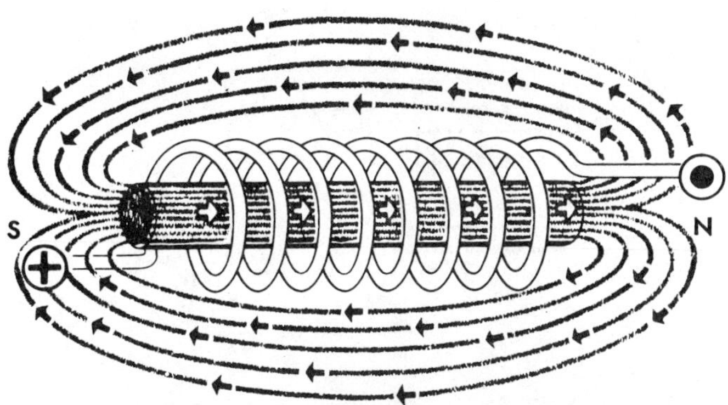

Fig. 2-7. Adding a soft-iron core to increase the strength of the electromagnet.

It would take considerable current flowing through the conductor in Fig. 2-5 to produce a reasonably strong magnetic field. However, if we took a number of conductors, all of which had the current flowing in the same direction, the individual magnetic fields would add up to produce a substantial magnetic flux. We can create this condition simply by winding a single conductor into a coil of many turns. Fig. 2-6 shows such a coil which is called an *electromagnet.*

By placing an iron core within this coil, as illustrated in Fig. 2-7, the magnetic strength of the electromagnet is increased. The rotor coil of an alternator is wound on a similar iron core. Soft iron is used because it will not retain much magnetism (called residual magnetism) when the coil current is turned off. If a harder iron were used, it would tend to become permanently magnetized, even after the coil current was cut off. This, of course, would defeat the purpose of the electromagnet, which is to allow us to control the strength of the magnetic flux produced by it.

HOW A SIMPLE ALTERNATOR WORKS

Alternators, as well as generators, work because of the principle known as *electromagnetic induction.* We saw in the first chapter that there are three requirements for alternators and generators to produce or generate an electrical current. The first requirement was a magnetic field, the second was a current-carrying conductor (winding), and the third was motion. The motion between the magnetic field and the conductor cannot be in just any direction; the conductor must cut the magnetic field perpendicularly or at right angles to the magnetic lines of force. If the conductor moves parallel to these lines of force, no current will be generated.

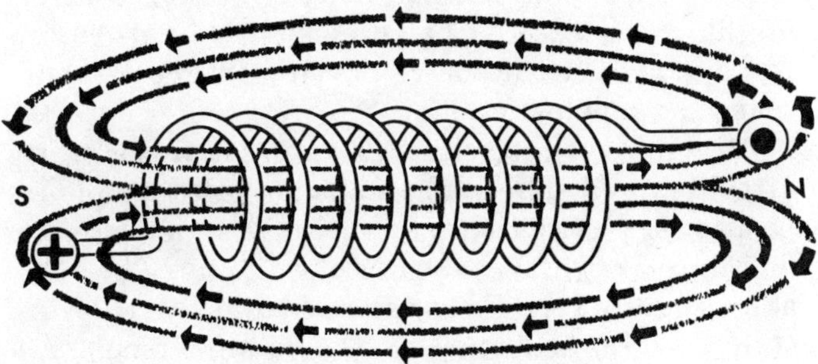

Fig. 2-6. A basic electromagnet.

Fig. 2-8 shows the basic elements necessary to generate an electrical current (a voltage reading indicates that a current is flowing). Notice that the conductor is moving *across* the lines of magnetic flux. As a result, current is induced in the conductor. The same thing would happen if the conductor stood still and the magnetic field moved across the conductor. But notice in Fig. 2-9 that the relative motion is *parallel* to the magnetic field. As a result, no current is induced in the conductor.

A very important point to remember about the relative motion between the conductor and the magnetic field is that when the direction of the motion is reversed, the induced current also reverses.

Now that we know what is required to produce or generate an electrical current, let's see how

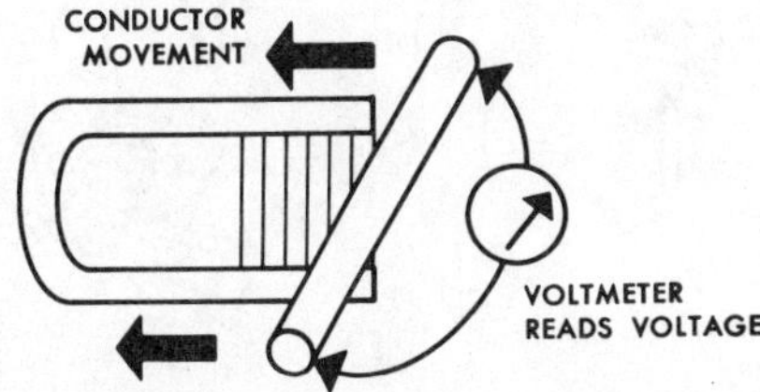

Fig. 2-8. A conductor cutting across a magnetic field.

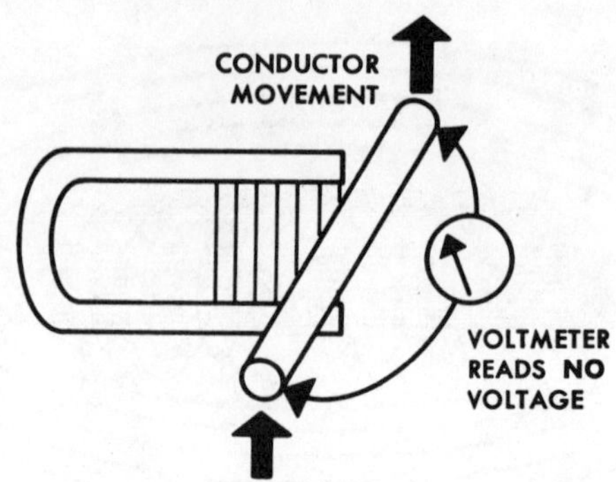

Fig. 2-9. A conductor moving parallel to a magnetic field.

this is put to use in a basic alternator. In the simplified version shown in Fig. 2-10, the stator winding consists of a single turn. The rotor, instead of being an electromagnet, is simply a single permanent magnet with one north and one south pole. As the magnetic field of this permanent magnet rotor revolves, the lines of magnetic flux cut the stationary conductor that forms the stator winding. This induces a current in the stator winding as shown in the upper portion of Fig. 2-10.

However, when the rotor has made half a revolution, its north and south poles will reverse. This has the effect of reversing the *direction* of the motion of the magnetic field. As a result, the current induced in the stator winding also reverses as shown in the lower illustration of Fig. 2-10. When the rotor returns to its former position, the induced current will again reverse.

> NOTE: Studies of electron movement have revealed that electrons actually flow from negative polarity to positive polarity rather than from positive to negative as assumed under the old current theory. However, for many years most instrument applications and rules for determining the direction of a magnetic field have been based on the old conception. For this reason, all illustrations in this book showing current movement have been made to agree with the old current theory in order to avoid confusion. All references to current flow or magnetic field direction are based on the current theory, unless specifically stated otherwise.

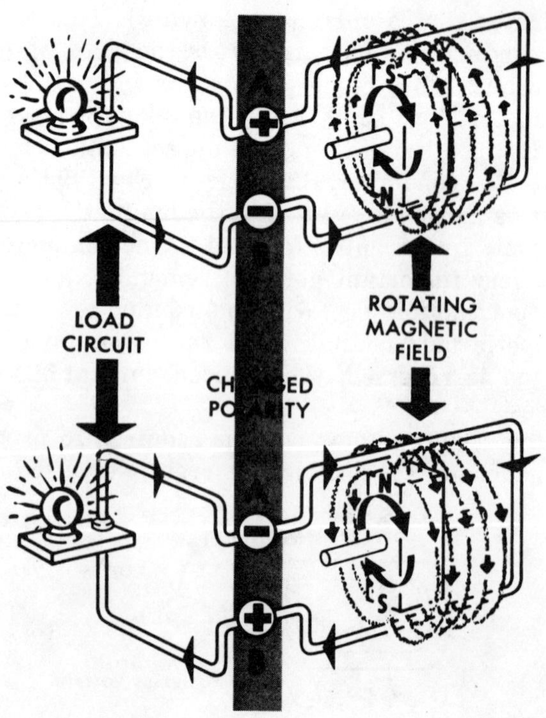

Fig. 2-10. A basic alternator generating an ac current.

THE THREE-PHASE ALTERNATOR

Although a simple alternator such as we have described would supply current to the battery, it wouldn't work efficiently. To improve efficiency, that is, the power output, all modern automotive alternators are built on the *three-phase* design. In effect, a three-phase alternator is basically three, single-phase alternators assembled into one unit. Actually, only the stator and the rectifier assembly are three phase; the rotor, which supplies the rotating magnetic field, is common to all three phases.

To see how these three phases work together to produce a smooth, continuous output current, let's consider first the current developed in just one phase. Refer to Fig. 2-11. For simplicity, this particular phase winding of the stator is shown as a single turn of wire, as indicated by the two small circles at the top and bottom of the stator frame. Also for simplicity, the rotor contains but two poles, a north and a south pole. In reality, a rotor might contain 12, 14, or 16 poles. A 14-pole rotor, for example, would have seven north poles and seven south poles.

Assume that the rotor is rotating in a clockwise direction, and that at a particular instant it is in position 1. Notice that none of the rotor's magnetic flux lines are cutting the stator winding. The voltage generated in the stator winding at this instant is zero, as shown by the voltage graph. As the rotor continues to turn, the south pole of the

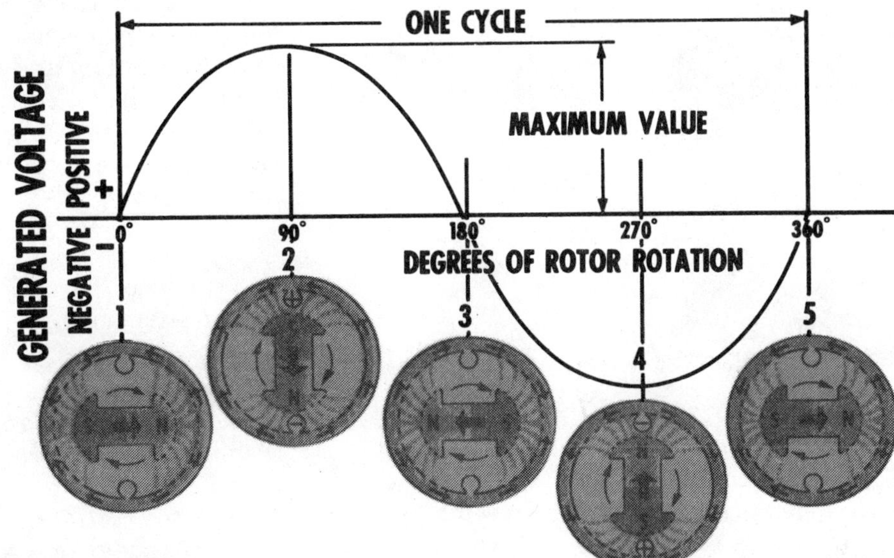

Fig. 2-11. Voltage generated in one complete cycle of the alternator.

rotor approaches the upper turn of the stator winding and the north pole likewise approaches the lower turn. As the rotor approaches position 2, the voltage generated in the stator winding increases in the positive direction due to the increased magnetic flux.

When the rotor passes position 2, the flux density decreases as does the induced voltage. By position 3, the rotor is in the same relative position as in position 1, except that the poles are reversed. As the rotor approaches position 4, the voltage generated in the stator again reaches a maximum, but this time in the opposite or negative direction. Position 5 shows the rotor in the same position it was in in position 1. This sequence of events constitutes *one cycle* of generated voltage.

Notice that the generated voltage is alternating; first, it increases to a maximum positive value, decreases to zero, and then increases to a maximum negative value. The voltage graph shown in Fig. 2-11 is called a *sine wave*. You would see exactly the same type of sine wave if you were to plot the voltage at a wall outlet. The voltage at the wall outlet is said to alternate at a rate of 60 cycles per second, or at 60 hertz (one hertz equals one cycle per second).

The frequency of the voltage produced by an automotive alternator is not constant. It depends on the speed of the rotor, which is a function of engine speed, and also on the number of poles in the rotor. Fig. 2-12 shows a typical rotor containing 14 poles. It consists of two 7-fingered cups, between which is sandwiched the rotor coil that supplies the magnetic field. One cup forms all the south poles and the other cup forms all the north poles. When assembled, the fingers interleave, creating alternate north and south poles. The rotor coil winding terminates at two slip rings.

Since in this example there are, in effect, seven separate magnets, each of the three stator windings will have seven sets of coils, all connected in series. Each coil contains a number of turns of wire. Fig. 2-13 shows a stator assembly with the windings for only one phase installed.

There are two methods of connecting the three stator windings. The first method, called the *wye* (Y) connection for obvious reasons, is shown in

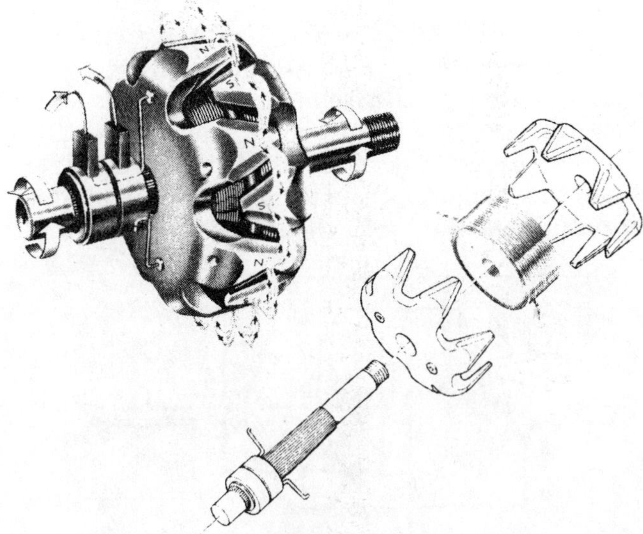

Fig. 2-12. A typical rotor assembly for an alternator.

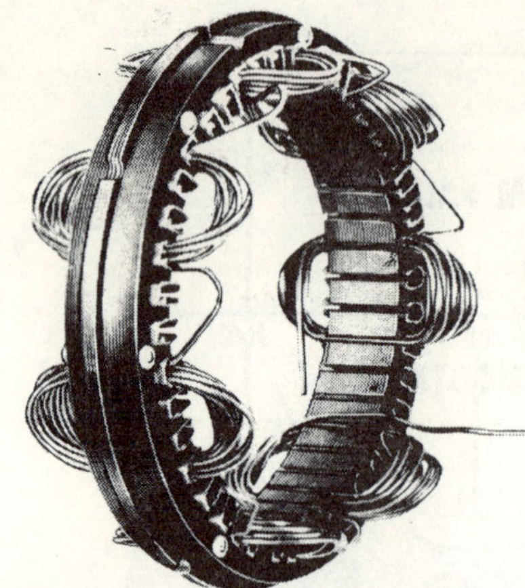
Fig. 2-13. A stator assembly showing the windings installed for only one phase.

Fig. 2-14. The second method is called the *delta* connection after the Greek letter it resembles. The delta connection is shown in Fig. 2-15. From an engineering standpoint, there are technical reasons for selecting one or the other type of connection. However, these reasons need not concern us here. For our purposes, it makes little difference which type of connection is used. Each type is tested and serviced in the same manner.

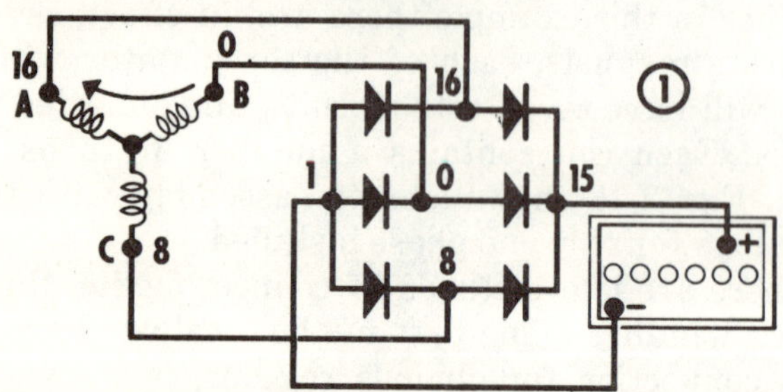

Fig. 2-14. A stator winding employing the wye connection.

However, it should be mentioned that the wye connection can develop a problem normally not associated with the delta connection. The point where the three stator windings join, sometimes called the *neutral point,* can oxidize or become open. When this happens, the alternator cannot produce an output current, even though the rotor and the rectifier assembly test normal. The only practical way to verify such a condition is to disassemble the alternator and visually inspect the neutral point. A bad neutral point will generally show signs of overheating or burning. This problem can sometimes be corrected by cleaning and soldering the connection.

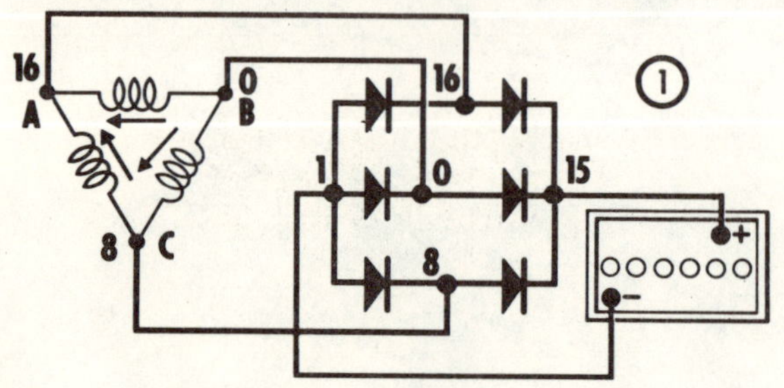

Fig. 2-15. A stator winding employing the delta connection.

RECTIFICATION

As we have seen, the current generated in the stator windings is *alternating current.* For this reason, alternators sometimes are called ac generators. However, an automobile's electrical system requires *direct current* (dc). To convert the alternating current of the stator into direct current requires a *rectifier.*

In the older dc generators rectification was accomplished mechanically by the commutator bars and brushes. In the modern ac generator, or alternator, this function is performed by a system of *diodes.* This diode system sometimes is called a rectifier assembly, although you will frequently hear them referred to simply as diodes.

A diode can be thought of as a one-way electronic valve. Current can flow through this valve in one direction but not the other direction. If we assume current to flow from a positive source to a negative source, then current will flow through a diode in the direction shown in Fig. 2-16. The diode symbol is that of an arrow striking a target; the arrow side is called the *anode* and the target side is called the *cathode.*

If the voltage applied to the anode is positive and that applied to the cathode is negative, the diode is said to be *forward biased.* This means that it is in its *conducting* state and current can pass through it as shown in Fig. 2-17A. But if the voltage should be reversed (Fig. 2-17B), the diode is *reversed biased* and no current can pass.

In summary then, current can pass through the diode in only one direction. This means that the current passing through the load (shown by the resistor symbol in Fig. 2-17) is dc or direct current. If the coil shown in Fig. 2-17 represents a

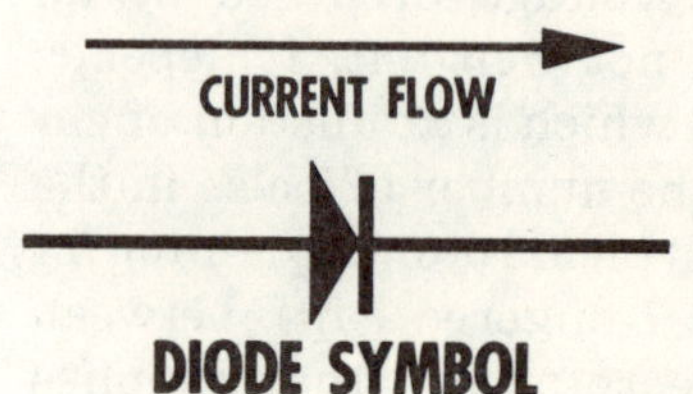

Fig. 2-16. Diode symbol and direction of conventional current through diode.

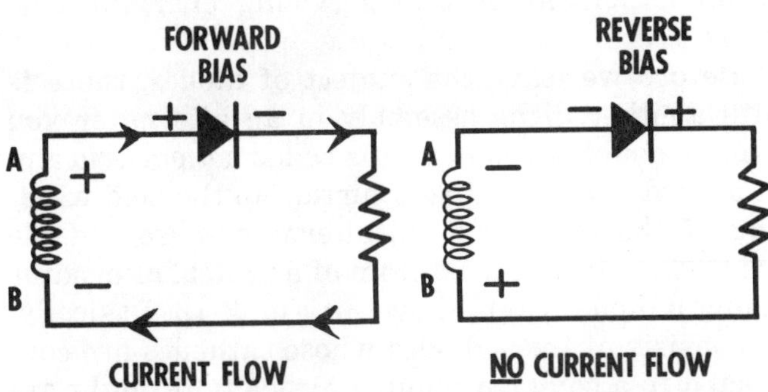

(A) Diode forward biased.
(B) Diode reverse biased.

Fig. 2-17. Bias voltage on a diode.

stator winding in which an ac current is generated (see Fig. 2-11), it will be apparent that current will flow through the load only half the time. The other half of the time, when the stator voltage is reversed, no current will flow. This is called *half-wave rectification.* It is not a very efficient arrangement for an alternator.

To improve efficiency, an alternator uses a diode arrangement that is known as a *full-wave* rectifier. The principle of a full-wave rectifier is shown in Fig. 2-18. By tracing the arrows in this illustration, you can see that the direction of current flow in the load is always in the same direction. Notice that no matter whether the voltage of the stator winding is positive or negative, there will always be a flow of unidirectional current through the load. In other words, there will always be direct current flowing in the load. (The load could represent the vehicle's battery or any other electrical device.)

The direct current produced by the full-wave rectifier is not a smooth or constant current, but rather a pulsating or rippling current. However, when we combine the rectified outputs of all three stator windings, we find that the output current of the alternator approaches that of an almost pure direct current.

The actual diode configuration used in a three-phase alternator is shown in Figs. 2-14 and 2-15. This particular arrangement is known as a *three-phase, full-wave bridge rectifier.* Practically all alternators, regardless of manufacturer, use this type of rectifier. The differences are mainly in the method by which the diodes are mounted on their heat sinks. (A heat sink is a piece of metal with a large surface area for the purpose of dissipating the heat caused by the current flowing through the diode.) In some alternators, the diodes are

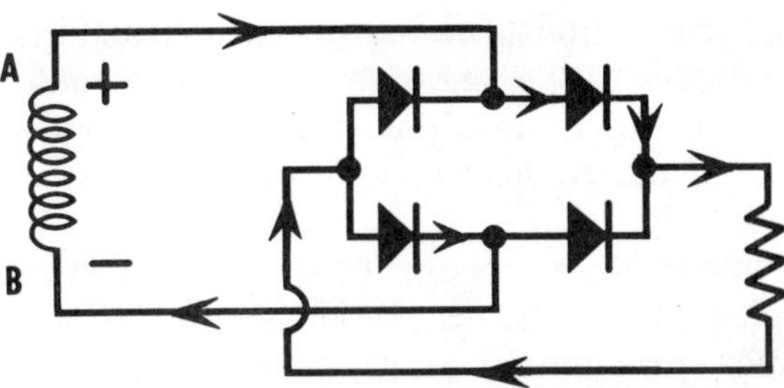

(A) Voltage at top of stator winding is positive.

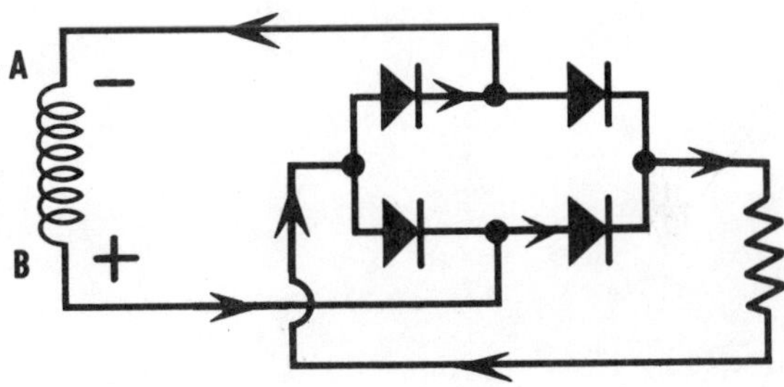

(B) Voltage at top of stator winding is negative.

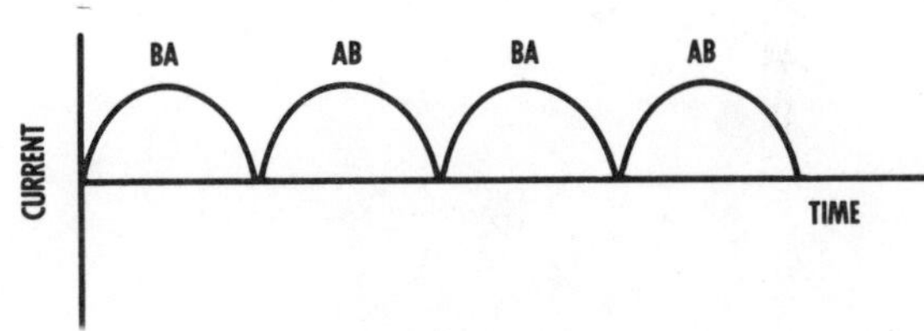

(C) Current output.

Fig. 2-18. A full-wave rectifier assembly for one stator winding.

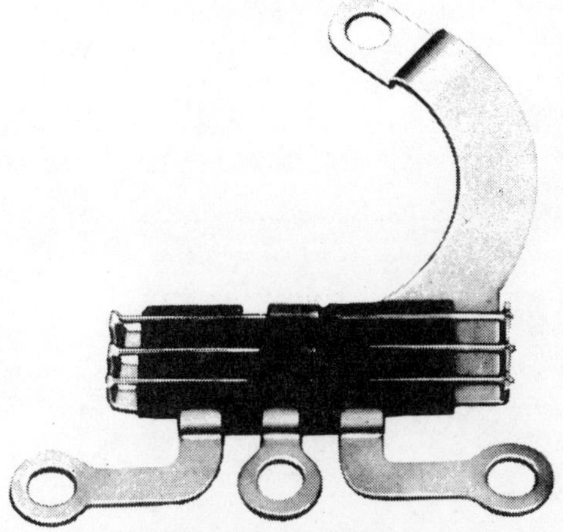

Fig. 2-19. A typical diode trio.

individually replaceable. In others, the diodes are permanently attached to their respective heat sinks; three diodes to the positive heat sink and three diodes to the negative heat sink. Should only one diode fail in an alternator employing this design, the entire heat-sink assembly must be replaced.

In later chapters we will discuss the testing and replacement of diodes. Diode failure is a fairly common problem in alternators. Theoretically, a diode should not fail since it has no moving parts to wear out. However, experience tells us otherwise. Knowing what symptoms a faulty diode can produce and the techniques for spotting such problems is an important part of servicing charging systems.

Before we leave the subject of diodes, there is still another diode assembly in an alternator you will no doubt encounter. It is called a *diode trio* and it is used to supply direct current to the field winding of the rotor. Not all alternators use a diode trio. The schematic diagram of a typical alternator using a diode trio is shown in Fig. 3-12. Basically, it consists of three diodes whose cathodes are connected to a common point. Physically it might appear as shown in Fig. 2-19. The individual diodes are electrically the same as the main rectifier diodes, although they are usually smaller since they do not have to carry heavy currents.

CHAPTER 3

Alternator Regulators

If an alternator were to be operated without any form of regulation—that is, with full system voltage applied to the field coil—its voltage would rise to dangerously high levels, especially if the electrical load were light. A heavy electrical load, such as a discharged battery, would temporarily hold the voltage down until the battery came up to full charge. But once the battery approached full charge, the voltage would continue to rise until it became high enough to overcharge the battery and reduce the life of various electrical accessories. The operating life of headlamps and other lights is considerably shortened by high system voltages.

For this reason, an alternator must be provided with some form of voltage limitation or regulation. The regulator, in effect, puts a limit on the amount of voltage that an alternator can produce. By doing this, the charging current supplied to the battery and the current demanded by the other accessories will be self-regulating. As we will see in the next section, the battery actually regulates its own charging current.

CHARGING CHARACTERISTICS OF BATTERIES

In order to properly analyze charging-system complaints, it will be helpful to understand some of the characteristics that affect the charging of the battery. Although there are a number of factors affecting battery charging, we are going to concern ourselves with only the major ones. Primarily, these consist of: (1) state of battery charge, (2) battery temperature, and (3) battery condition.

It may surprise you to learn that it is actually the battery itself, and not the voltage regulator, that regulates the amount of charging current. This is not to say that the regulator does not play an important role in this process. Naturally it does. But as you will see, the regulator can do only so much—the rest is up to the battery.

In order for a battery to receive a charging current, it must be connected to a current source (the alternator) that is at a higher voltage than the battery voltage. In other words, there is a difference between the battery voltage and the alternator voltage. It is this voltage *difference* that actually regulates the battery's charging current. The voltage of the charging source, the alternator, is controlled by the voltage regulator as explained elsewhere. For the purpose of this discussion, let's assume that the alternator voltage is held or fixed at some constant level.

But what about the battery voltage? What determines this value? Basically, there are two factors involved. The first is called CEMF for *counter-electromotive force*. It is also referred to as *chemical voltage* since it is produced mainly by the chemical reaction within the battery. This is the voltage that must be overcome by the alternator voltage before charging can occur. See Fig. 3-1. The second factor is called the battery's *IR drop,* since it is caused by the internal resistance of the battery. If you recall Ohm's law, you will remember that I (current) times R (resistance) equals E (voltage). Therefore, IR drop is simply a voltage measurement.

If you add these two voltages together, CEMF and IR drop, you will get the battery's charging voltage. This is the voltage you will measure when you connect a voltmeter across the battery terminals while it is under charge. Depending on various factors, it may or may not be equal to the voltage regulator setting, as shown in Fig. 3-2. Note that the charging voltage of battery "A" never

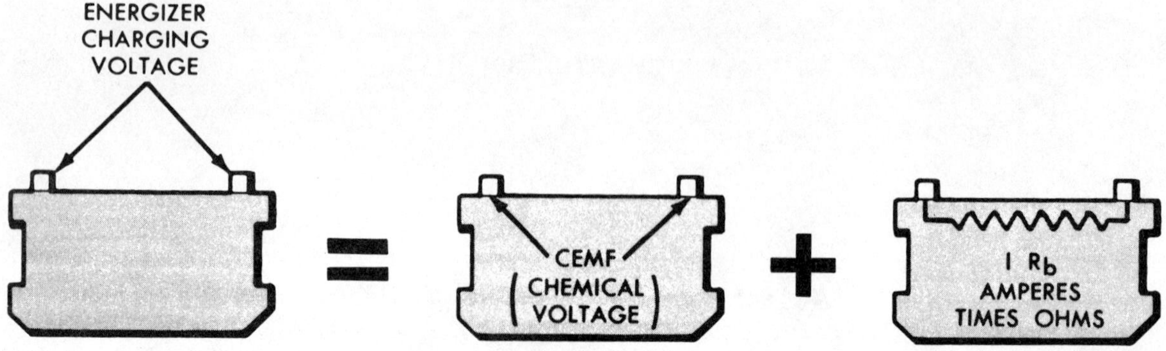

Fig. 3-1. A battery's charging voltage is equal to its CEMF plus the voltage drop caused by the internal resistance of the battery.

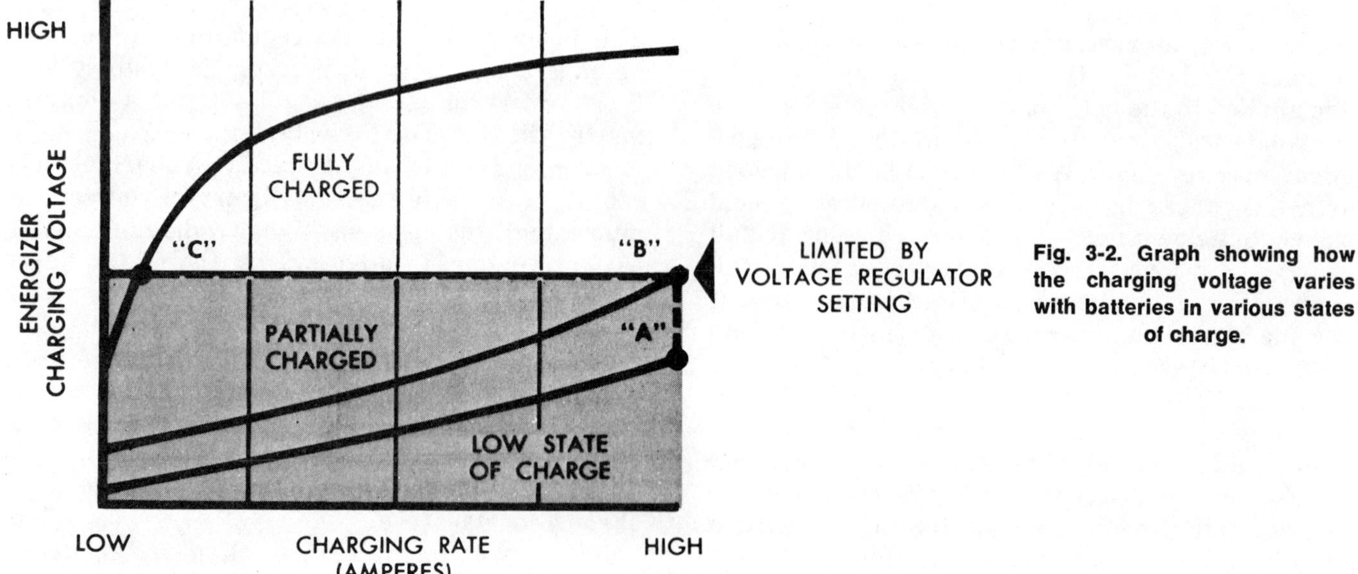

Fig. 3-2. Graph showing how the charging voltage varies with batteries in various states of charge.

reaches the level of the voltage regulator; the charge rate is limited by the maximum output of the generator.

The CEMF is affected by not only the chemical action of the battery, but also by the concentration of the electrolyte (its specific gravity), temperature, charging rate, plate area, condition of the electrolyte, age, and gassing. Gassing is the natural byproduct of charging as evidenced by the formation of oxygen and hydrogen at the positive and negative plates respectively. The effect of these gasses, chiefly hydrogen, is to raise the battery's CEMF. However, it is the concentration of the electrolyte, which indicates the state of charge, that has the most pronounced effect on CEMF. This is shown in Fig. 3-3.

The battery's IR drop also is controlled by a variety of factors. The I of the IR drop is the charging current itself. The R represents the battery's internal resistance and is made up of the normal resistance of the internal connectors and plate material plus the resistivity of the electrolyte. The resistance is quite temperature-sensitive due, primarily, to the electrolyte. As the temperature drops, electrolyte resistance increases, as does the

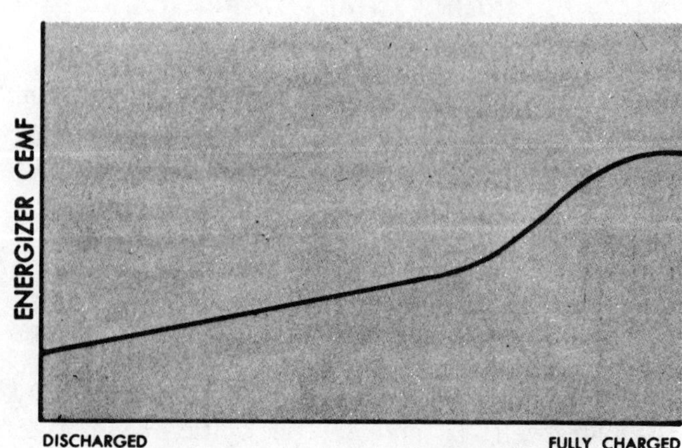

Fig. 3-3. CEMF of battery increases with state of charge.

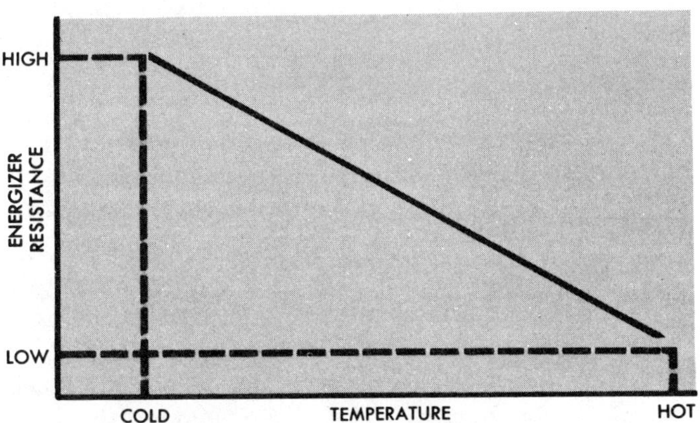

Fig. 3-4. Internal resistance of battery decreases as its temperature rises.

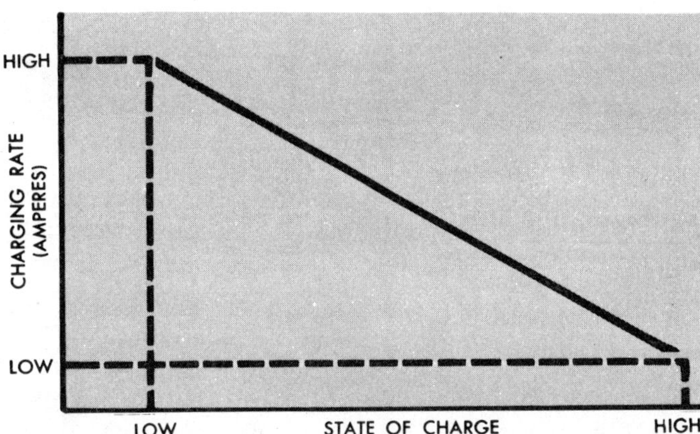

Fig. 3-5. The charge rate of a battery automatically tapers off as its state of charge increases.

CEMF. What this means in terms of charging current is that the charge rate decreases as the temperature goes down. In other words, it is harder to charge a cold battery than a warm one. This is shown in Fig. 3-4.

This is evident from the charging-voltage formula:

$$\text{Charging Voltage} = \text{CEMF} + \text{IR drop}$$

Let's say the charging voltage, which can be considered the voltage-regulator setting, remains constant. If the CEMF and R (the battery's internal resistance) increase due to lower temperatures, then I (charging rate) must *decrease* to balance the equation.

Most voltage-regulators are temperature compensated so that their control voltage is higher at lower temperatures. Just how this is accomplished is explained later in this book. The important thing to remember, though, is that it is necessary to take into account the temperatures of the regulator and the battery when measuring voltage-regulator settings.

When the battery is in a low state of charge—that is, when the electrolyte concentration (specific gravity) is low—the CEMF will also be low. Looking again at the charging-voltage formula, you will see that I (the charge rate) must *increase* to balance the formula. As the battery charges and the specific gravity increases, the CEMF also increases. To maintain formula balance, the charge rate must now *decrease* as shown in Fig. 3-5. This means that the charge rate automatically tapers off as the battery charges. Thus, all other factors being equal, it is the battery itself that regulates its own charge rate.

There is one situation in which the battery's charging voltage may be below the voltage-regulator setting. This is when the battery is in a very low state of charge or when the battery has just been subjected to a heavy, sustained discharge such as prolonged cranking. Under these conditions, of course, the CEMF will be low. The IR drop will also be limited due to the maximum output current of the alternator. In other words, the charge rate (I) cannot exceed the maximum output of the alternator; the battery is taking the full alternator output when it is in a low state of charge. Under these conditions, the charging-voltage formula will yield a value below the voltage-regulator setting. A voltmeter connected across the battery at this time will show a voltage somewhat less than the actual voltage-regulator setting. As we have mentioned before, don't be fooled into thinking that this voltage represents the setting of the regulator.

Another situation to watch for is the case of a sulfated battery. Lead sulfate is a substance that forms naturally on the positive and negative plates as the battery discharges. It then disappears, being reconverted into acid and lead, as the battery charges. This represents the normal chemical action of the battery. The problem with lead sulfate is that if it is not soon reconverted to acid and lead by the recharging process, it will harden on the plates. When this happens, it becomes almost impossible to reconvert it to acid and lead by recharging. The battery has then become *sulfated.* Among other things, the insoluble lead sulfate reduces the effective area of the plates, and thereby reduces the actual electrical capacity of the battery.

This lead sulfate, once it has hardened, also increases the battery's internal resistance (R). This means that the charging rate (I) must decrease to balance the charging formula. Even though the battery is in a discharged condition—a sulfated battery can never be fully charged—its charge rate will be low. It is limiting its charging rate as though it were fully charged. If you experience a situation where the specific gravity and the charge rate are both low, but the charging voltage normal, you may have a sulfated battery.

The most common cause of sulfation is allowing a battery to remain in a discharged or partly discharged condition for a period of time without recharging. It is hard to say just how long a discharged battery can remain uncharged before sulfation causes a problem. Experience seems to indicate that if the discharged period extends beyond several weeks, irreversible sulfation may start to set in. The best way to prevent this condition is to make sure that the battery is always maintained at full charge. A fully charged battery cannot sulfate.

THEORY OF REGULATION

Although the trend is toward solid-state voltage regulators, electromechanical (or vibrating) voltage regulators are still being used and will be around for many years. For this reason, we will begin our discussion of alternator voltage regulators with the vibrating type. Once you have a good understanding of how a vibrating voltage regulator functions, it should be a simple step to understanding the operation of solid-state voltage regulators.

Just how does a voltage regulator regulate an alternator? How is it able to maintain the voltage of an alternator at approximately the same level under a wide variety of operating conditions? It does this job by controlling the alternator's field current. As we saw earlier, the output current of an alternator is controlled, in part, by the amount of field current flowing in the rotor. Reduce the field current and you reduce the alternator output current. This, essentially, is what the voltage regulator does. However, the way it does it may not be the way you might think.

The regulator does not control the alternator field current in a smooth, continuous manner such as the way a faucet regulates the flow of water. Rather, the regulator performs its control function by switching the field current on and off. Because it does this so rapidly, the *effect* is that of a smooth, continuous control of the field current.

The rate at which the regulator switches the field current on and off varies, depending on operating conditions, from a few cycles per second to several hundred cycles per second. By following exactly what happens during one of these cycles, you will get a good idea of how a voltage regulator operates.

We will take first a simple, single-contact regulator and then move on to the slightly more complicated, double-contact regulator. A single-contact regulator is shown in Fig. 3-6. Consider the regulator to consist of two main sections: (1) the voltage-sensing section and (2) the field-control section. The voltage-sensing section "senses" when the alternator's voltage approaches the desired control level. When this occurs, it causes the field-control section to reduce the alternator's field current suddenly. This, in turn, causes the alternator's output current, and hence its voltage, to drop. When the voltage drops below the control level, the voltage-sensing section again allows the field-control section to permit full field current to flow into the alternator's rotor.

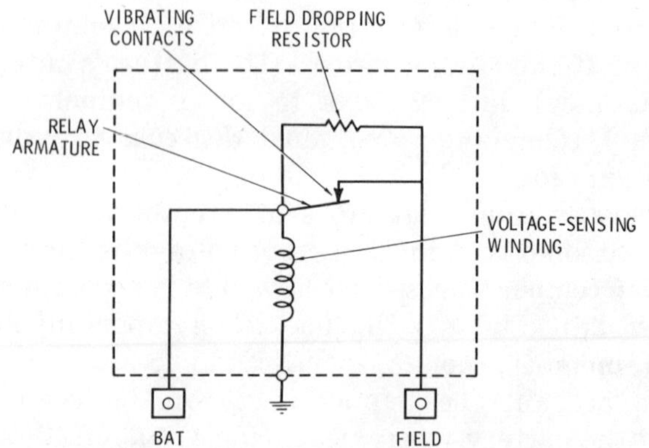

Fig. 3-6. A single-contact voltage regulator.

In a simple vibrating regulator, the voltage-sensing section consists of the winding on the core of the regulator. Note in Fig. 3-6 that this winding is connected between ground and the output side of the alternator. Whatever voltage is developed by the alternator will be impressed across this winding. Since it consists of many turns of fine wire, the winding draws little current. However, it is still an electromagnet and when enough voltage is impressed across the winding, its magnetic strength will be sufficient to pull down the relay armature immediately above it.

The contacts that form the field-control section of the regulator are on the relay armature. When system voltage is low, this armature is held in the up position by spring tension. This closes the regulator contacts, and thus allows full field current to flow from the alternator (or battery) through the field winding of the rotor. This mode, of course, permits the alternator to produce its full output and, as a result, the alternator voltage begins to rise rapidly.

But as the alternator voltage rises, the magnetic pull on the relay armature increases. At some predetermined voltage level (controlled by the spring tension on the armature), the voltage-sensing winding has enough magnetic attraction to overcome the spring tension on the armature. The relay contacts open and field current is diverted through a current-limiting resistor. This reduces the field current and consequently the alternator voltage drops. When the voltage drops below the preset level, the armature spring closes the contacts and again allows full field current to flow. The alternator voltage again increases and the whole cycle repeats itself.

Just how rapidly this process repeats itself depends primarily on alternator speed—actually, engine speed—and the battery's state of charge. If the alternator speed is high and the battery is at full charge, the voltage-regulator relay may open and close (vibrate) as often as several hundred times a second. On the other hand, at low speeds or conditions of low battery charge, the frequency may be only a few times a second—or the relay may not cycle at all. Another factor affecting the operating frequency of the regulator is the fact that the alternator output cannot change instantaneously. It takes a small faction of time, measured in milliseconds, for the alternator voltage to increase or decrease.

We have seen how a simple alternator regulator functions by switching field current between two levels: full field current and reduced field current. However, under certain conditions of high speed and very light electrical loads, merely reducing field current may not be enough to prevent alternator voltage from rising above the desired level. A simple regulator such as we have just described could lose control of the alternator voltage at high speeds with a light load. What is required under these conditions is not merely to reduce the field current to some low value, but to reduce it to zero.

This can be accomplished with a double or dual-contact voltage regulator, which is the type most commonly used when a mechanical regulator is employed to control the alternator. Essentially, it is the same as the simple, single-contact regulator just described but with an additional contact added. A dual-contact regulator is shown in Fig. 3-7.

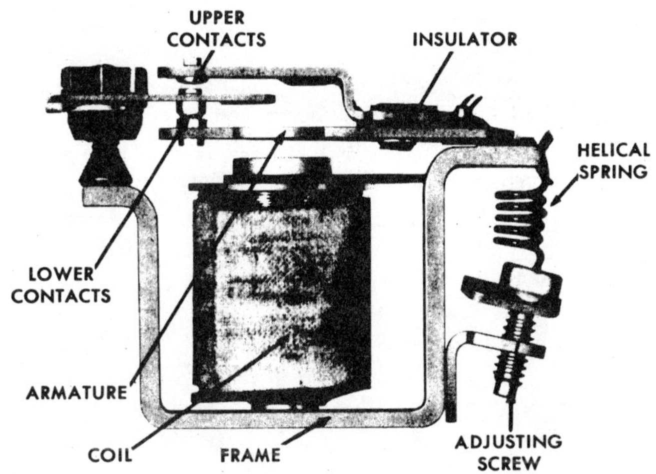

Fig. 3-7. A typical dual-contact voltage regulator.

The purpose of this extra contact is to ground the field (or rotor) winding when alternator output voltage tends to rise above the desired control level. By grounding the field winding, field current is reduced to zero, thus reducing the alternator output also to zero. To see just how this extra contact functions, we will trace the regulator's action through a typical cycle of operation. Refer to Fig. 3-8. Assume that the engine speed is high and that the electrical load is merely a few amperes, as it would be with a fully charged battery and no electrical accessories turned on.

At first, the armature of the regulator relay will be in the up position, held there by the tension of the armature spring. The lower contacts are closed when the armature is in this position, connecting the field directly to the alternator's output. The resulting full field current causes the output of the alternator, and consequently its voltage, to increase. As the alternator voltage rises to the preset level (controlled by armature spring tension), the relay armature will be pulled downward, causing the lower contacts to separate. Because the field current must now flow through a resistor, it decreases. This, in turn, reduces the alternator output.

However, if the alternator speed is high enough and the load light enough, even this reduced field

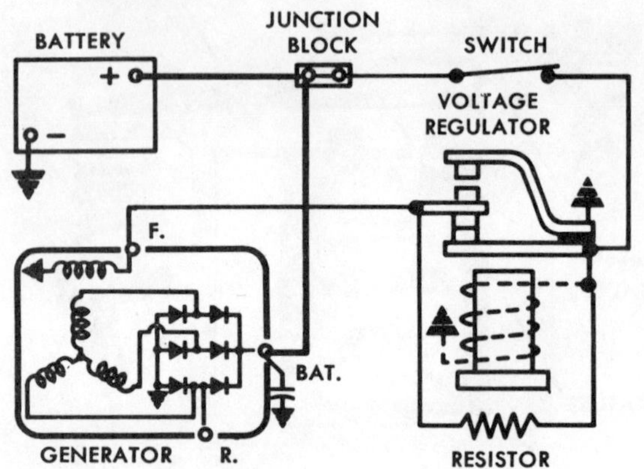

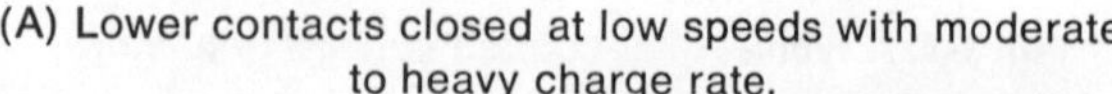
(A) Lower contacts closed at low speeds with moderate to heavy charge rate.

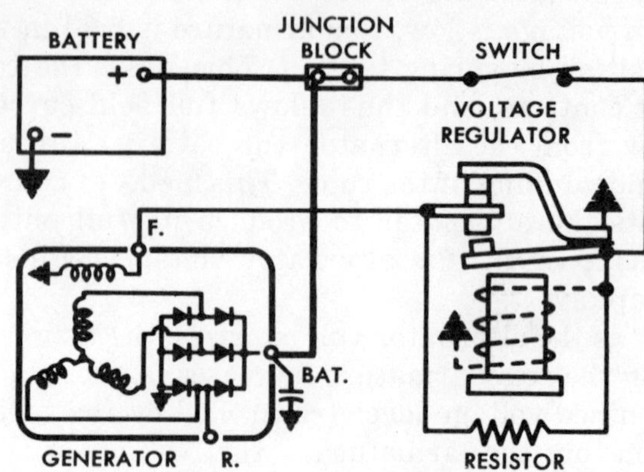

(B) Upper contacts closed at high speeds and light loads.

Fig. 3-8. Two basic operating modes of the dual-contact regulator.

current may be too high to control the alternator output voltage. As a result, the output voltage will tend to rise above the desired level. But when this happens, the relay armature is pulled downward even more and the field contact makes connection with the grounding contact. Since both ends of the field winding are now at ground potential, this prevents any field current from flowing. With no field current, the alternator can produce virtually no output; its voltage drops and therefore voltage regulation is maintained. Just as it did with the single-contact regulator, this cycle repeats itself many times a second.

From the standpoint of testing and adjusting there is little difference between the single-contact and the dual-contact regulator. The same servicing procedures can be used for both. But regardless of which type regulator is used—and this applies to solid-state regulators as well—it is very important to make certain that the regulator is actually in operation when it is being tested. Contrary to popular belief, the regulator is not always regulating (operating to control the alternator output) just because the engine is running.

For example, if the engine speed is low and the electrical load is high, possibly due to a discharged battery, the regulator may not be functioning. Even though full field current is flowing, the combination of low speed and the high current demanded by the battery may be enough to hold alternator voltage at or below the preset regulator voltage. If you attempt to measure the regulator voltage under these conditions, you would get an erroneous value since the regulator is not operating. This is illustrated graphically in Fig. 3-2.

There are several things you can do to prevent yourself from falling into such a trap. First, be sure that the charging current is at a low level as measured with a test ammeter. The current should be well below the maximum output level of the alternator being tested. If you do not have a test ammeter, make certain the battery is at or near full charge by testing it with a hydrometer. Also, keep the engine speed at or above the minimum test speed, usually 1500 to 2000 rpm. If the voltage continues to climb, wait until it levels off before taking your final reading.

Some charging-system testers have a special ¼-ohm resistor that is inserted into the main charging system during voltage-regulator tests. The purpose of this resistor is to make a discharged battery look like a fully charged one. This "tricks" the regulator into operation so that accurate regulator settings can be measured regardless of battery condition. This is a handy device but it is not essential if you observe the precautions just discussed.

SOLID-STATE REGULATORS

In principle, solid-state regulators differ little from the previously discussed electromechanical regulators. They control alternator output by switching field (rotor) current on and off at a rate determined by the alternator speed and load. It makes no difference whether an alternator is being controlled by an electromechanical (vibrating) regulator or by a solid-state regulator.

Solid-state regulators offer several advantages over vibrating types, but they also have what some may consider to be disadvantages. Their main advantages are longevity and the ease with which they can be miniaturized. This latter advantage has led to the development of the integral charging system in which the regulator is incorporated within the alternator. This has created what amounts to a single-unit charging system. We will discuss the integral charging system later in this chapter.

Because solid-state regulators contain no vibrating contacts, which eventually wear out due to electrical erosion, they can theoretically last indefinitely. However, solid-state devices themselves (diodes, transistors, etc.) are not failure-proof and when one fails, the whole regulator fails. Because most solid-state regulators are potted or otherwise sealed, the defective component cannot be replaced; the complete regulator must be replaced. This, some service technicians feel, is a disadvantage, since vibrating regulators can often be repaired simply by dressing the contacts. Also, they point out, the voltage setting of a vibrating regulator can be adjusted by varying the tension of the armature spring. Most solid-state regulators have a fixed voltage setting that cannot be changed.

Whether these objections are bona fide or simply a reluctance to accept new technologies, is a moot question. The fact remains that solid-state regulators, as well as a host of other solid-state products, represent a growing trend in modern automotive design. Although there is little you do in the way of servicing these units, it is very helpful from a troubleshooting standpoint to know how these devices function.

Going back to our original breakdown of a regulator into (1) a voltage-sensing section and (2) a field-control section, we find that this applies also to the solid-state regulator. The voltage-sensing section is controlled by a device called a *zener diode*, and the field-control section utilizes a *power transistor*.

The transistor acts as a switch to turn field current on and off. It serves the same function as the relay contacts in a vibrating regulator. But because there is no contact arcing, the transistor can turn the field current from fully on to fully off, thus maintaining complete alternator control over the full range of speeds and electrical loads. The transistor performs the same function as the double-contact regulator.

Fig. 3-9 illustrates how the transistor accomplishes this switching action. The terminals labeled *emitter* and *collector* form the main current-carrying path through the transistor. This is the path through which the field current flows. The *base* terminal can be considered the control input. When no current flows into the base terminal, the resistance between the collector and emitter terminals is very high. Virtually no current will flow through the collector-emitter circuit and the transistor is said to be in its *off* state. This means that no field current can flow and, therefore, the alternator output is zero. The off state of the transistor can be likened to the open-contact state of the vibrating regulator.

However, by injecting a small control current into the base circuit, the resistance of the collector-emitter circuit can be made very low. The transis-

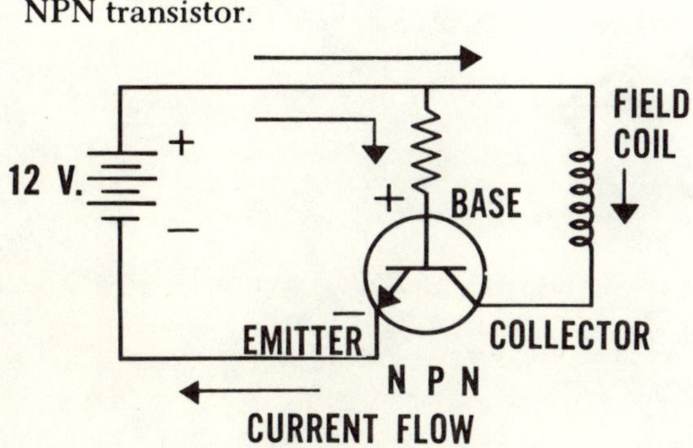

(A) Emitter-base forward biased.

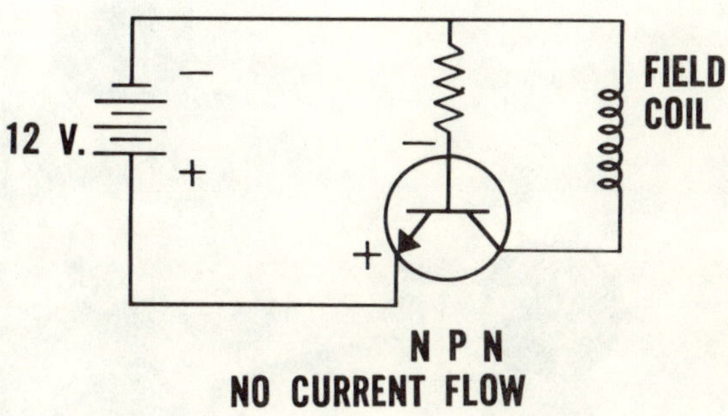

(B) Emitter-base reverse biased.

Fig. 3-9. Basic principle of field-current control in a solid-state regulator.

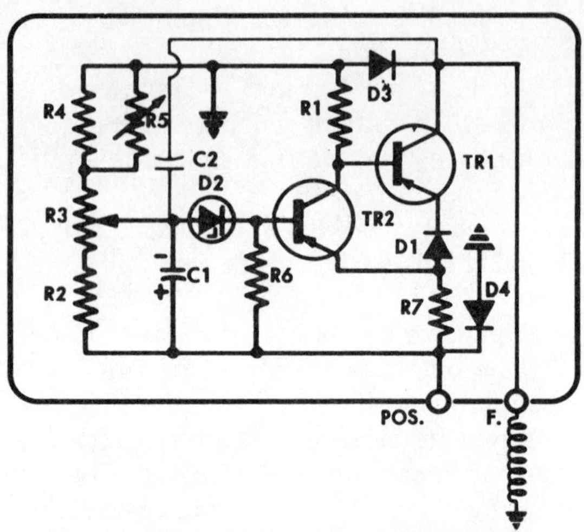

Fig. 3-10. Typical solid-state voltage regulator.

tor is now in its *on* or conducting state. In this state, full field current will flow and alternator output will increase toward its maximum level. Again, the on state of the transistor can be compared to the closed-contact state of the vibrating regulator.

By switching the transistor between its on and off states, the field current, and consequently the alternator output, can be controlled to whatever level we desire. But what controls the transistor? How is it made to turn on and off at the proper time? This is the function of the zener diode, or rather the voltage-sensing section of the regulator.

A zener diode is a special type of diode. A conventional diode, as we saw in the previous chapter, will pass current in the forward direction but block it in the reverse direction. A zener diode behaves much like a conventional diode, but only up to a point. It passes current in the forward direction and blocks it in the reverse direction—until a certain reverse voltage is reached. When the reverse voltage reaches a given level (determined by the

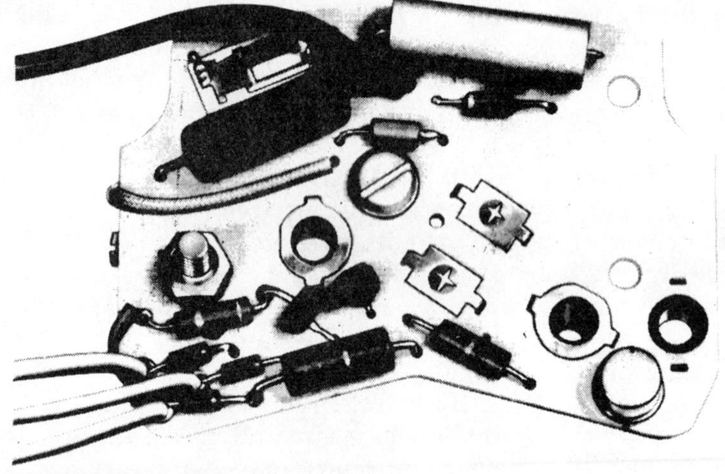

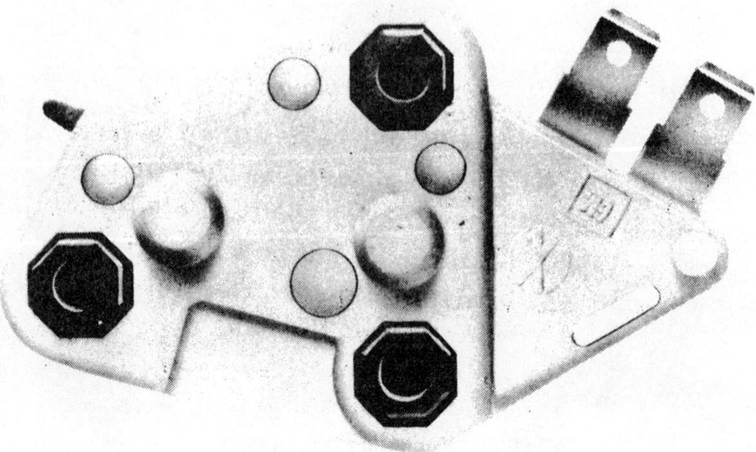

Fig. 3-11. A solid-state regulator designed to be installed within an alternator.

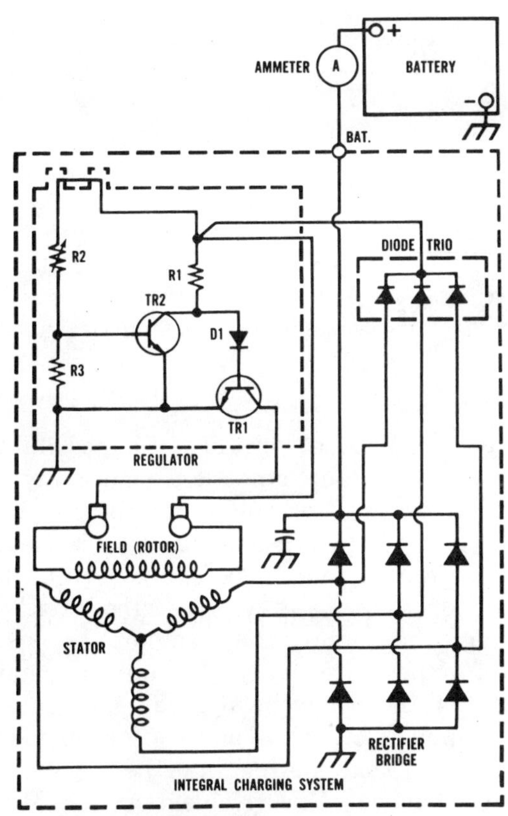

Fig. 3-12. A simplified circuit diagram of an integral charging system.

zener manufacturing process) the zener diode suddenly begins to conduct. In a conventional diode, this would be considered a breakdown and would probably destroy the diode. But no harm occurs in a zener diode due to its particular design characteristic.

Because of this unique characteristic, the zener diode becomes a voltage-sensing device and, hence, the heart of the solid-state regulator. The zener does not control the power transistor directly, but, instead, controls it through a *driver* transistor. Notice in Fig. 3-10 that the zener (D2) connects to the base terminal of the driver transistor (TR2). As long as alternator voltage remains below a certain level, the zener does not conduct and no base current flows into the driver transistor. This puts the driver transistor in the off state. Due to the way in which the driver transistor is connected to the power transistor (TR1), when the driver transistor is in the off state, the power transistor is in the on state.

This allows full field current to flow and, as a result, the alternator voltage begins to rise. When this voltage reaches a predetermined level, the zener diode suddenly becomes conductive. The current through the zener diode flows into the base of the driver transistor and puts it into the on state. When the driver transistor is on, the power transistor is off. This interrupts the field current and alternator voltage falls off. When voltage falls below the preset level, the whole regulator cycle starts over again. Thus, the alternator voltage remains *regulated* at the desired charging-voltage level. Just how rapidly this regulation cycle repeats depends on alternator speed and electrical load as it did with the vibrating regulator.

You must observe the same precautions when testing charging systems with solid-state regulators as you did with vibrating regulators. Also, the methods of testing and the instruments used are the same regardless of which type of regulator is used. We will cover specific testing and troubleshooting procedures in the next chapter.

THE INTEGRAL REGULATOR

As mentioned earlier, the solid-state regulator permits a degree of miniaturization that allows the regulator to be physically incorporated into the alternator. Such a regulator is shown in Fig. 3-11. Other than this physical difference, though, the integral charging system is electrically equivalent to a charging system using external regulators. From a functional and diagnostic standpoint, both systems may be treated alike. The simplified circuit of an integral charging system is shown in Fig. 3-12.

The only disadvantage to the service technician is that it usually is not so easy to substitute a suspected regulator when troubleshooting an integral charging system. In most instances, it is necessary to remove the alternator to gain access to the regulator. In some cases, it may be necessary to disassemble the alternator. This means that a greater reliance must be placed on test instruments and proper test methods rather than on substitution techniques. You will want to be quite certain that the problem actually lies in the alternator-regulator unit before you go to the trouble of removing it.

CHAPTER 4

On-the-Vehicle Testing

The purpose of the charging system can be summed up rather simply—to keep the battery fully charged. And we might be tempted to add—to supply the current to operate all the various electrical accessories. But this latter requirement is secondary to the task of maintaining the battery charge. If the battery cannot be maintained in a fully charged state, the charging system is not doing the job it was designed for, regardless of any other considerations. Of course, if the battery itself is defective, we have an entirely different type of problem.

In this chapter we are going to be concerned with two things: (1) the causes of charging-system troubles and (2) how to detect them. First, let's consider what types of charging-system problems we are likely to encounter.

TYPICAL CHARGING-SYSTEM PROBLEMS

Charging-system troubles can be categorized into three main groups:

1. No charging current.
2. Low charging current.
3. Excessive charging current.

There is no particular order as to which type of problem is most likely to develop. The first type of problem, that of *no charging current,* is the most easily recognized. Either the alternator warning light comes on or the ammeter (if the vehicle is so equipped) shows discharge. If, for one reason or another, the car owner is unaware of or ignores the normal warning indication, the battery eventually runs down and results in a "no-start" condition.

Almost anything in the charging system can cause a no-charging-current problem. The most obvious trouble is a broken or badly slipping fan belt. Always check the fan belt first. Although not a frequent source of trouble, the possibility of broken wires or bad connections, especially at the alternator output terminal, can be easily and quickly checked. In other words, check the easily inspected trouble sources before you go on to the more elaborate tests we will describe later.

Among the items that cannot be visually checked, experience seems to indicate that the regulator, rather than the alternator, is more commonly responsible for no-charge situations. This is not to suggest that the regulator be routinely substituted whenever this problem arises. We will describe more positive ways of pinpointing the trouble a little later. In the case of integral charging systems, substitution is not always accomplished easily and, therefore, you will want to be quite certain where the trouble is before taking this step.

Let us now turn our attention to the second group of charging system troubles, that of *low charging current.* This problem is closely related to the previous problem and is sometimes mistaken for it. In fact, the end result of either type of trouble if allowed to progress, is the same—a dead battery.

Again, the cause could be as simple as that of a loose or slipping fan belt. Even with nearly proper belt tension, a glazed belt can slip enough to cause a charging problem, particularly during periods of heavy electrical loads such as nighttime winter driving. Make it a regular practice to check the condition and tension of the alternator drive belt. Although an experienced service technician can judge approximate belt tension by feel, the practice is not recommended. Special gauges are available for this purpose and should be used. Proper belt tension is more critical than many realize. For example, too much tension can and does lead to early alternator bearing failures.

However, before you begin troubleshooting the charging system, make sure that you actually *have* a problem of low charging current by checking the battery's specific gravity. If it is not up to full charge levels—the specific gravity varies from 1.250 to 1.275 depending on the battery manufacturer—you probably have a low-charging-current problem. The battery's specific gravity is one of the best indicators of charging-system condition available to you. Remember at the beginning of this chapter we said that the purpose of the charging system is to keep the battery fully charged. If the system fails to do this, there is something wrong. (Note that certain types of maintenance-free batteries do not permit access to the electrolyte and, therefore, the specific gravity cannot be checked. In these instances, you will have to rely on voltage and current measurements for determining charging-system condition.)

The causes of low charging current are as varied as those for no charge current. Poor wiring can contribute to the problem but is not a common occurrence. If the system utilizes an electromechanical (vibrating) regulator, the cause may be as simple as a misadjusted armature spring. A charging-voltage test will quickly reveal such a condition. Because of the nature of semiconductor devices, which generally either work or don't work, solid-state regulators seldom get out of adjustment. A common alternator trouble is that of a shorted diode. Just one shorted diode can reduce alternator output by 50 percent or more. This is more than enough to create a charging problem, especially when electrical loads such as headlights are in use.

Strangely enough, an open diode has much less effect on alternator output. Unless you use specialized test instruments, such a problem may go undetected, even with standard testing procedures. However, since alternator diodes seem to have a greater tendency to short than to open, open diodes are not a common problem. In fact, in cases of dire emergency where a replacement alternator or diode assembly is not available, it is possible to "convert" a shorted diode to an open diode simply by cutting the diode lead wire. This will restore the alternator to nearly normal operation, although it should be considered, at best, only a temporary expedient. Of course, to do this, you must first know which diode is shorted. This will be discussed in the next chapter.

In the last group of charging system problems, that of *excessive charging current,* we have an entirely different situation. One of the most insidious aspects of this problem is that it frequently goes unnoticed until after other problems develop. These other problems are chiefly shortened battery life due to damaged plates and shortened headlamp life.

The battery is the best indicator of such a condition, other than an actual voltage measurement. If the battery seems to be using an excessive amount of water, it is probably due to excessive charging. There is an exception, however. Under conditions of abnormally high operating temperatures—summer driving in hot climates—a battery will tend to consume more water than normal. But the mere fact that a battery needs water is not, by itself, an indication of excessive charging current. All batteries, except maintenance-free types, require periodic water replacement. As a rule, normal water consumption is about one ounce of water per cell per 1000 miles.

About the only practical way to detect excessive charging levels is with a voltmeter. A high charging voltage coupled with high water consumption in the battery is a fairly positive indication of excessive charging current. The cause is most generally confined to the regulator. But it can also be caused by poor wiring, particularly poor grounding of the regulator itself. If the regulator is a vibrating type, the problem usually can be solved by simply reducing the voltage regulator setting (reducing the spring tension on the regulator armature). Normally, a reduction of only a few tenths of a volt is all that is required. Since most solid-state regulators are nonadjustable, the only solution is a new regulator.

Don't overlook the effect of a poor regulator ground in cases of excessive charging current. Some regulators rely solely on the mounting screws to effect the proper ground connection. Others use a separate wire to ensure good grounding. But in either case, a poor regulator ground circuit can cause the charging voltage to be higher than the actual voltage-regulator setting. A high charging voltage means a high charging current.

So far, we have discussed the basic types of charging-system problems and their most usual causes. Although the various symptoms we have described—principally those obtained from the battery—are good indicators of charging trouble, the only way to be absolutely certain is with the use of test instruments. These can be as simple as a voltmeter or as complex as a specially designed charging-system analyzer. Properly used, a voltmeter can supply you with a good deal of information about the charging system. Here are some simple troubleshooting methods that can be performed with a minimum of test equipment.

QUICK TROUBLESHOOTING TESTS

One of the fastest and easiest checks you can make on any charging system, regardless of type, is called the *charging-voltage test.* It requires only a voltmeter, preferably one with a range of 0-16 or 0-18 volts. Most automotive voltmeters meet this requirement. Simply connect the instrument across the battery and operate the engine at a fast idle (1500 rpm or higher). First leave all accessories off and let the voltmeter reading rise until it levels off. This will be the charging voltage. It should generally be between 13.4 and 15.0 volts when the system is at its normal operating temperature.

If the charging voltage is below this range, there is most probably a charging-system problem. If the voltage remains at the battery voltage level, approximately 12.6 volts, the charging system probably is not working at all. But before you make a decision, let the engine run at fast idle for a minute or two to see if the charging voltage starts to climb. With a discharged battery, it is possible for the charging voltage to remain temporarily low until the battery picks up a charge. One good way of eliminating this possibility is to check the battery's specific gravity. If it is reasonably high, say above 1.225, and the charging voltage remains low, you can be quite certain that you have a charging problem.

If the charging voltage is within the desired range of 13.4 to 15.0 volts, and the battery at or near full charge, the charging system *probably* is good. To be absolutely sure would require a more detailed testing procedure, including an alternator output test.

If the charging voltage is above 15.0 volts, there is a good possibility of excessive charging current, especially if the battery is low on water. Be sure, though, that the system is at normal operating temperature. It is normal for a regulator to operate at a higher voltage when it is cold than when it is warm. As a general rule, 10 minutes or more of operation will bring the system close to its normal operating temperature range. Naturally, if the vehicle has just been driven, you can assume that normal operating temperatures have been reached.

So far, we have checked the system with all accessories off, the only load on the alternator being that of the battery and, of course, the ignition system. The second phase of the voltmeter check requires that all major accessories be turned on. This part of the check is performed only if the previous voltage readings were in the normal 13.4 to 15.0 range.

Turn on the high-beam headlights, the blower motor to high speed, the air conditioner, and the windshield wiper motors. Hold engine speed at about 2000 rpm and note the voltmeter reading. It is normal for the charging voltage to drop somewhat from the no-load reading, but it should still remain above battery voltage by about 0.5 volt or more. Since the battery voltage is normally about 12.6 volts, this means that the charging voltage under load should not go below a minimum of 13.1 volts.

If the charging voltage does drop to approximately the battery voltage, it indicates that the alternator output cannot meet the demands of the accessory load. This frequently means a faulty alternator, although the problem could be simply a slipping drive belt. The fact that the no-load voltage reading was normal usually indicates that the regulator is working properly. However, there is always the possibility that the regulator is partially defective.

BYPASSING THE REGULATOR

The charging-voltage test can actually be performed in much less time than it takes to describe it. Although it is a simple check, it can yield a lot of information about the charging system when properly performed and intelligently evaluated. We can even carry the process a step further by repeating the test with the regulator *bypassed.* This procedure should be done only if the no-load charging voltage reading is *below* the normal range.

When you have this situation, the problem could be either a defective regulator or a faulty alternator. Bypassing the regulator is one way of finding out which one is at fault. When the regulator is bypassed, the alternator is operating, or should be operating, without any voltage limiting. If the charging voltage rises above battery voltage with the regulator bypassed, but not otherwise, you can be quite certain that the regulator is defective. On

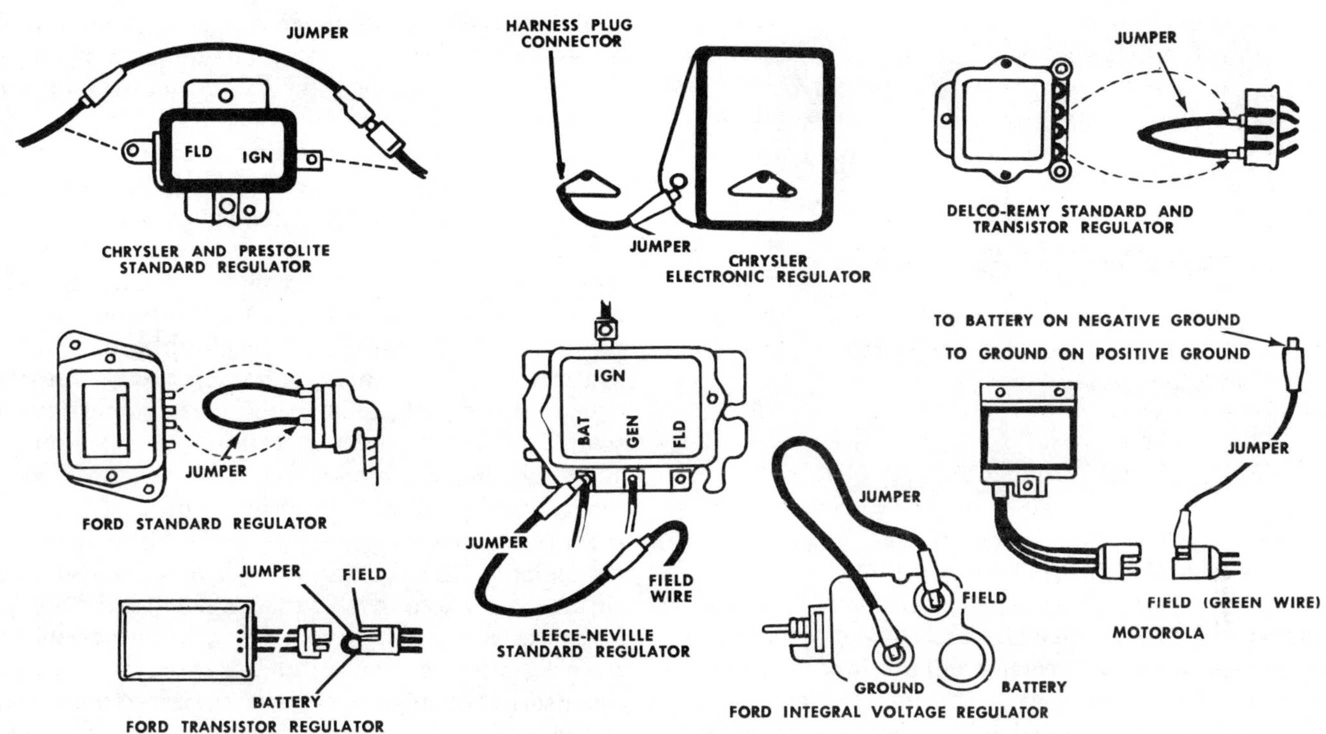

Fig. 4-1. Typical regulator bypass connections.

the other hand, if the voltmeter remains at the battery voltage with the regulator bypassed, the alternator is defective.

Basically, bypassing a regulator consists of connecting the alternator field terminal directly to ground or to the alternator output terminal, depending on the particular type of alternator being tested. Because of the many different makes of alternators, especially those on imported vehicles, it is difficult to give specific bypassing instructions. Fig. 4-1 shows bypass connections for most of the currently encountered domestic vehicles. If you are in doubt as to the proper connection, refer to the manufacturer's service manual. Remember, though, that when a regulator is bypassed, the alternator has no voltage control and its voltage can go quite high. Therefore, make the charging-voltage test as quickly as possible. Return the engine to idle as soon as you have noted the voltmeter response. Don't let the charging voltage go above 16 volts.

CHARGING-SYSTEM ANALYZERS

Although the voltmeter affords a simple and convenient way of making a quick check of the charging system, it cannot make the detailed tests required for a complete charging-system analysis. For example, it cannot measure the actual current output (amperes) of the alternator. Nor can it give a direct indication of diode condition. These and other test functions are contained in instruments that are commonly called *charging-system analyzers.*

Courtesy Marquette Mfg. Co.

Fig. 4-2. A combination generator, alternator, and regulator tester incorporating a field-control rheostat.

Courtesy Sun Electric Corp.

Fig. 4-3. A volt-ampere tester for testing the starter system as well as the charging system.

The simplest of the analyzers consist of nothing more than a volt-ammeter combination, with possibly a ¼-ohm resistance in the ammeter circuit to simulate a fully charged battery. The most elaborate versions contain, in addition, a variable carbon-pile loading device to simulate various electrical loads, a field-current ammeter, a field-current rheostat to control alternator output, and a dynamic diode test circuit for detecting faulty diodes without removing the alternator. Typical charging-system analyzers are shown in Figs. 4-2 and 4-3.

The specialized test functions of the more-elaborate instruments are handy features to have, especially for the charging-system specialist. The average service technician, however, can get along quite nicely with some of the less sophisticated versions, or even with a basic volt-ammeter. The secret of diagnosing charging-system troubles lies not so much in the instrument as it does in the technician using it. If you have a good grasp of charging-system theory and know how to make full use of your analyzer, you will be able to solve just about any charging complaint.

Because of the many charging-system analyzers on the market, it would be impossible to give even general test procedures for their use. Each manufacturer provides detailed, illustrated instructions on how to use his particular analyzer. There are a wide variety of instruments from which to choose, from small, hand-held units to large stand-mounted consoles. Although the larger units usually provide a few more test functions than the smaller instruments, price and size alone should not be the deciding factors. The amount of charging-system work you intend to do and the type of systems you will primarily be working on will dictate the type of analyzer best suited to your needs.

For passenger-car applications, a voltmeter range of 0-16 or 0-18 volts is sufficient. A low range, for instance 0-4 volts, is useful for voltage-drop tests but is not absolutely necessary. The ammeter range should be at least 80 amperes and preferably 100 amperes. Some of the more elaborate testers offer dual ranges up to 400 amperes or more. These higher ranges are generally intended for starter-system tests or for high-output charging systems such as found on buses and large trucks. A dynamic diode test circuit is frequently included in the charging-system analyzer and is a very handy thing to have. It gives a positive indication of diode and stator condition and helps to pinpoint problems involving these components. Before you decide on an analyzer, carefully study the literature of the various manufacturers and compare features. But remember, even the most elaborate instrument, if improperly used, cannot compare to the most basic instrument in the hands of a skilled operator.

A new type of charging-system analyzer has recently appeared on the market. Its distinguishing features are small size and the use of lights, rather than a meter, to indicate charging-system problems. These analyzers are easily connected to the system and are intended mainly for quick checks.

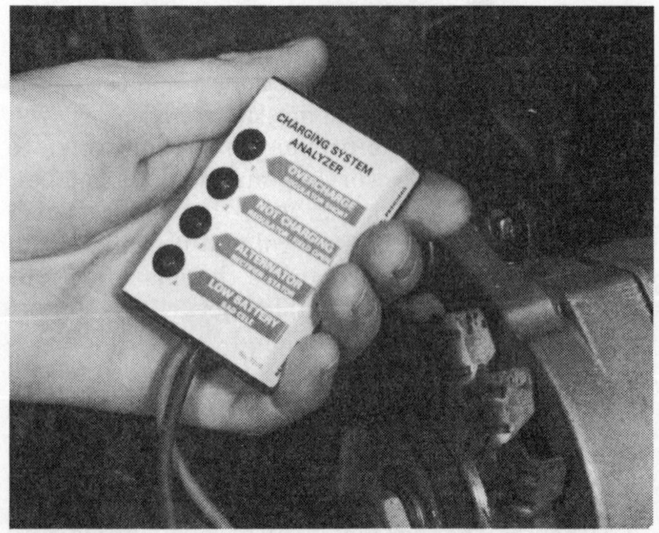

Courtesy Delco-Remy Div.

Fig. 4-4. A charging-system analyzer that uses lights to indicate specific problems.

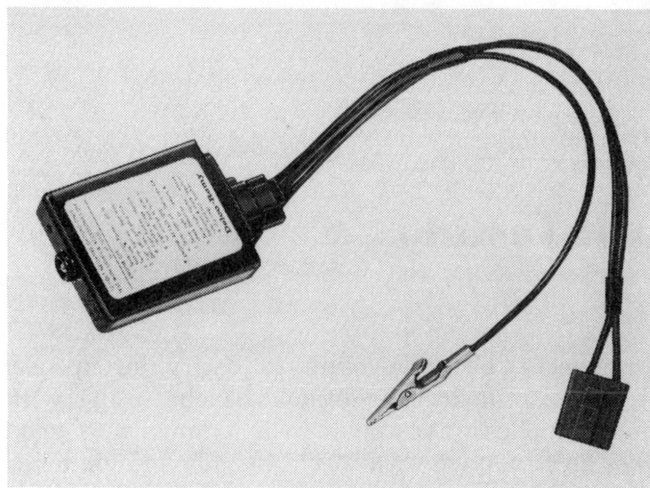

Fig. 4-5. A charging-system analyzer used to test Delco-Remy Delcotron alternators.

Although they are not as versatile as the standard analyzers previously mentioned, and cannot check out all facets of the charging system, they do a good job in spotting the most common troubles. Figs. 4-4 and 4-5 show typical units of this type. Because specific charging problems are indicated by lights, there is no interpretation involved in the use of these analyzers. This is a big help to those with little training in troubleshooting charging systems, but can also be useful to the charging-system expert.

The unit shown in Fig. 4-4, for example, has four lights, each indicating a specific problem. Only two connections to the alternator are required. The top or No. 1 light comes on if the charging voltage is too high (overcharging). The No. 2 light comes on if the charging voltage is too low, indicating a no-charge condition. The No. 3 light is a diode-stator indicator. If this light comes on, there is a shorted diode or stator winding. The bottom or No. 4 light provides a quick check of the battery. If the battery voltage under a headlight load is too low, the No. 4 light will turn on. This would usually be caused by a bad battery cell.

A similar analyzer is shown in Fig. 4-5. This particular unit is designed solely for use with Delcotron Generators (alternators). Although it has only one light, this analyzer performs essentially the same function as the previous instrument. Although these units can provide quick answers to specific charging-system problems, they should not be considered substitutes for complete charging-system analyzers. They can frequently be a timesaver by eliminating the need for a full charging-system test procedure in cases where there is no complaint of charging performance.

CHAPTER 5

Alternator Bench Testing

There are two schools of thought on alternating servicing. One approach holds that if the problem is confined to the alternator, it should be replaced, either with a new or a rebuilt unit. The other approach maintains that most alternator problems are generally of a minor nature and, once the trouble has been pinpointed, are easily repaired. Unfortunately, we cannot give any clear-cut guidelines as to which is the best approach. A lot depends on the individual service technician or the policy of the shop doing the servicing.

Usually, it comes down to a question of economics and the skill of the service technician. The cost of removing and replacing an alternator is the same whether it is to be replaced with another unit or whether the original unit is to be repaired. The question then becomes one of how much, in terms of labor and parts, will it cost to repair the unit as compared to replacing it. This is where a working knowledge of bench-testing procedures comes in handy. In many cases, it is actually more profitable to repair or rebuild an alternator than simply to replace it. Then again, a quick bench diagnosis may reveal that the best course is a complete replacement.

The purpose of this chapter is to describe briefly some easy bench-test procedures and some test instruments so that you can decide what might be the best course to take in any particular case. Remember, though, that certain bench tests will require the disassembly of the unit and that this sometimes necessitates special tools. However, the few special tools that you may need can quickly pay for themselves if you do any amount of bench servicing.

As for the necessary test instruments, these can cover the range from a simple test-light lashup to an alternator test bench costing $2000 or more. The latter, of course, would be only for those who have or expect to have the volume to justify the expense. You can still do considerable bench testing with just a modest investment in instruments. A good test unit to start with would include an ohmmeter with a high- and low-ohm range and an in-circuit diode tester. Sometimes these functions are combined into one test instrument and sometimes they are incorporated into an alternator test bench. Keep in mind that the purpose of a test bench is for determining whether an alternator does or does not meet specifications; it does not always aid in pinning down the exact cause of the problem. This is the job of the above-mentioned test instruments.

For the discussion to follow, we will assume that the alternator has been removed from the vehicle because it is reasonably certain that that is where the problem lies. This, of course, means that you have done a good on-the-vehicle diagnosis. If you are fortunate enough to have an alternator test bench, you can put it to good use in proving or disproving that the alternator actually is defective. Once the repairs have been made, the test bench should be used to verify that the unit is once again functional. If you do not have such a test bench, you can begin with the basic disassembled-alternator tests that we will describe shortly.

Before we go into specific tests, though, let's review the various trouble sources you are likely to find in a defective alternator. We will intentionally omit bearing trouble, since this is strictly a mechanical problem and its repair is obvious. Of the various electrical problems, that of a shorted diode is fairly common. The resulting symptom will be considerably reduced alternator output (or low charging voltage under full electrical load). This problem is quite easy to spot by various methods described in this chapter.

Another typical problem is an open field circuit, caused either by severely worn brushes or by an actual open in the rotor field winding. Again, this problem is easy to detect. Sometimes a break in the field winding occurs where the field winding connects to the slip ring. Resoldering the connection will frequently cure the trouble. In certain cases, a deposit will build up in the brush holder and prevent the brush or brushes from contacting the slip rings. The symptom caused by an open field circuit is complete loss of alternator output. A charging-voltage test will show low voltage, usually the battery voltage.

Shorted stator windings sometime occur. The symptom is basically the same as that of a shorted diode; that is, considerably reduced output. This type of trouble is normally found by process of elimination. If all the diodes check good, and there is evidence of overheating in one or more of the stator windings, it is usually safe to assume that a winding has shorted. However, be careful in judging overheated windings. A difference in the coloration of the windings is not always a sign of overheating. Since a stator normally has three different windings, it is not unusual to notice a difference in the color of the insulation. A better indication is the *fingernail test.* If the winding has been burned or overheated, the insulation can usually be flaked off with the fingernail. This will not happen with a normal winding.

Occasionally, you will find an alternator with an open wye (Y) connection. Naturally, this can occur only in alternators in which the stator windings are connected in the wye configuration. The symptom is the same as that of an open field circuit—no alternator output. Such a condition is best found visually. The wye connection point (where the three stator windings connect together) will usually appear charred and discolored due to overheating. In many cases, the connection will be loose. This condition can often be repaired by cleaning and recrimping (or soldering) the wye connection.

Although an alternator can develop other problems, those we have just discussed are the more common ones. As you can see, some problems are really quite simple and easily repaired. Others are more extensive in nature. In some alternators it is possible to replace just one diode; in others, they must be replaced in groups (or clusters) of three or six, even though only one diode is defective. Many alternators use a diode trio to supply the field current. These units, when defective, are replaced as a single component.

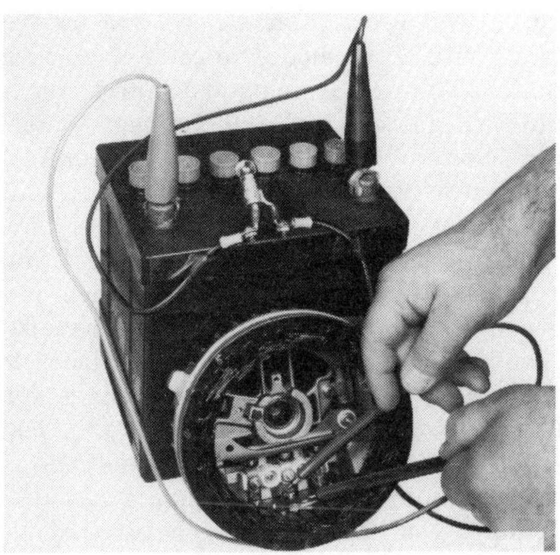

Fig. 5-1. An easily constructed diode checker.

Now, let's take a look at some of the instruments used in alternator bench testing. One of the simplest ones is a homemade affair consisting of nothing more than an automotive lamp in a suitable socket, some wire, and a battery. Such a tester is shown in Fig. 5-1. Similar devices, generally known as continuity checkers, are available from auto parts jobbers. With this device, you can detect shorted or open diodes. You can even check winding continuity in cases where you suspect an open field winding.

To show how this device can be used to check a diode, we will start first with a single diode that has been removed from an alternator or disconnected from the stator winding. We will show later how this can be done without removing the diodes. As illustrated in Fig. 5-2, connect one test lead to the diode case and the other to the diode pigtail lead, and then reverse the connections. If the diode is good, the light will come on with one connection but remain off with the other. If the diode is shorted, the light will remain on with *both* connections. If the diode is open, the light will remain off with either connection.

You can use essentially the same procedure for checking the diode clusters while they are still in-

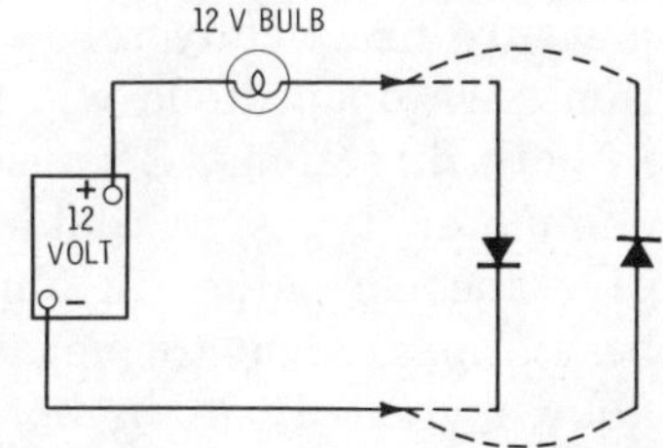

Fig. 5-2. Checking a diode that has been disconnected from the stator winding.

stalled in the alternator. There are two diode clusters (with three diodes in each cluster) in an alternator. The positive cluster connects to the alternator output terminal and the negative cluster connects to the alternator frame (assuming that the alternator is a negative-ground unit, which is the usual case). To check the positive cluster, connect one test lead to the output terminal and the other lead to any stator winding. Then reverse these connections. If the light remains on with *both* connections, one or more of the diodes in the cluster is shorted. Repeat this procedure for the negative cluster, only this time make your connections to the alternator frame and one of the stator windings. Again, if the light remains on with *both* connections, you have one or more shorted diodes. However, in order to pinpoint *which* diode is shorted, you must disconnect the stator windings and check each diode individually.

Unfortunately, the test-light device will not detect an open diode with this procedure. To check for this condition, it is necessary to disconnect the three stator windings from the diode clusters and test each diode individually as shown in Fig. 5-2. Open diodes, though, do not appear to be nearly as common as shorted diodes.

However, the test light does work quite well for checking field coil continuity in the rotor. Simply connect the test leads across the alternator's field coil terminals. (Note: One side of the field is often connected to ground.) If the light does not come on, there is a loss of continuity. This could be due either to poor brush contact on the slip rings or to an open field winding. To narrow down the source of the trouble, remove the brush holder or rotor assembly and connect the test leads directly to the slip rings. If there is still no light, the problem is an open field winding in the rotor. Additional uses for the test light will be described in later chapters that deal with specific alternator systems.

All of the foregoing tests can also be done with a suitable ohmmeter. Remember, a good diode will show low resistance with the test leads connected one way and very high resistance with the leads reversed. A shorted diode, on the other hand, will measure practically zero resistance in both directions. An open diode will show infinite resistance in both directions. Because of the many different ohmmeter types available, it is not possible to give specific values in ohms for diode tests. The best approach is to measure the resistance of a known good diode in both directions with your ohmmeter and record these values for future reference. Keep in mind, though, that the values measured with your instrument may not agree with those of a different instrument. Note also that the voltage at the probe terminals of some ohmmeters is too low to forward-bias a diode. In this case, a good diode will measure a very high resistance in either direction.

An ohmmeter is especially useful for checking the resistance of the field coil in a rotor. Fig. 5-3 shows such a test being made. The advantage of the ohmmeter is that you can get a specific resistance measurement—something you cannot do with a test light. This will not only show whether the field has continuity, but also whether the field has the proper resistance. Typical field-coil resistance is usually in the range of 3 to 6 ohms, although this can vary somewhat.

Manufacturers sometimes give the field-coil resistance directly in ohms, but usually it is given in terms of field current (amperes) at a certain voltage. This type of specification is easily converted to ohms merely by dividing the voltage by the field current. For instance, if the field current is given as 3.0 amperes at 12 volts, just divide the 12 volts by the 3 amperes and you will find that the resistance is 4 ohms. This is the approximate value you should measure with your ohmmeter.

A word of caution when using an ohmmeter to check field-coil resistance. Make this measurement directly on the slip rings. If you attempt to measure it through the brushes, you will probably

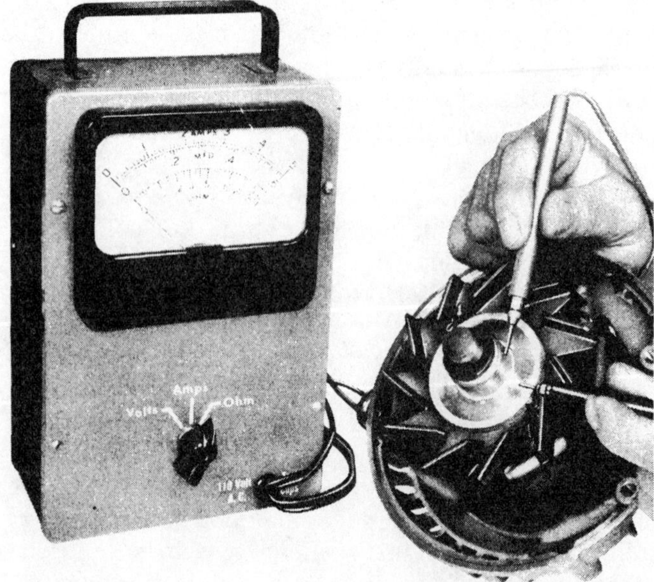

Fig. 5-3. Using an ohmmeter to measure field-coil resistance.

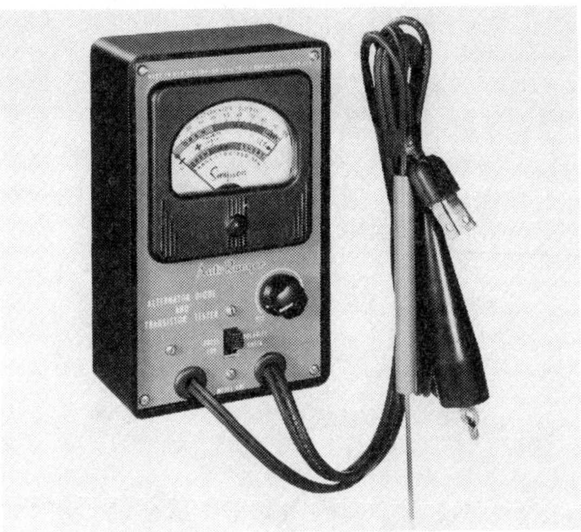

Courtesy Simpson Electric Co.

Fig. 5-4. An in-circuit diode tester that can be used to check diodes without disconnecting them from the stator winding.

get a false reading. Most ohmmeters, due to their low operating currents, will be affected by the contact resistance of the carbon brushes and will give erratic readings. But even an erratic reading is usually sufficient to show that there is at least continuity through the field coil.

A very handy instrument for alternator bench testing is the *in-circuit diode tester*. The advantage of such an instrument is that you can check diodes for both opens and shorts without disconnecting the stator windings. This is a big help when the windings are soldered to the diode clusters. A typical in-circuit diode tester is shown in Fig. 5-4.

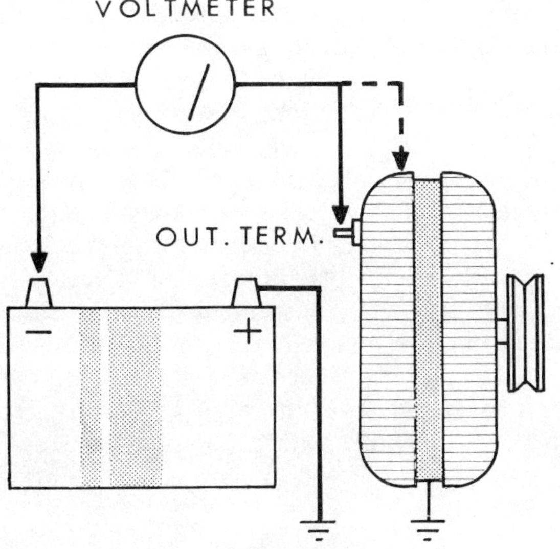

Fig. 5-5. Another method to check for shorted diodes without disassembling the alternator.

Most of these instruments require 115-volt ac power. A few diode testers also provide ohmmeter functions.

There is yet another way to check an alternator for shorted diodes. This method works on most units and has the advantage that it does not require the disassembly of the alternator. All you need is a battery and a voltmeter. In fact, this check can be made while the alternator is still on the vehicle if you first disconnect the battery cables and remove the wires from the alternator terminals. Fig. 5-5 shows this test method. Notice that the positive side of the battery is connected to the frame of the alternator. The voltmeter is connected as shown, first to the alternator output terminal and then to the alternator frame. Note the exact voltage reading with each connection. If the *difference* in voltage readings is approximately 1 volt, the diodes are not shorted. But if the difference is only about 0.5 volt, a diode is probably shorted.

So far, we have shown how to make most of the basic bench tests on an alternator. These are the tests that actually localize the problem to a particular component. Once the necessary repairs have been performed, we can only assume that the alternator is fully operable. If you have done a good job of testing and repair, the unit most probably is restored to normal operation. However, you can never be sure of this until you have reinstalled the alternator and made another on-the-vehicle test. If trouble still persists, you must determine if it is due to the alternator or if it is due to yet an additional problem in the system.

The best answer to this question is found in the bench-type alternator tester. This instrument allows you to fully check out an alternator after, or even before, repairs have been made. It permits you to test the unit under controlled conditions to see if it meets the manufacturer's specifications. When the alternator is installed in the vehicle you know for certain that it is working properly and any other trouble that may persist must be due to some other cause. These bench testers come in a wide variety of styles and prices. Fig. 5-6 shows a moderately priced tester that will check not only alternators but generators, and regulators as well.

As we mentioned earlier, bench testers of this type are not intended to specifically pinpoint the problem, but rather to make an overall test of the alternator. If the alternator does not come up to specifications, you must then proceed with the

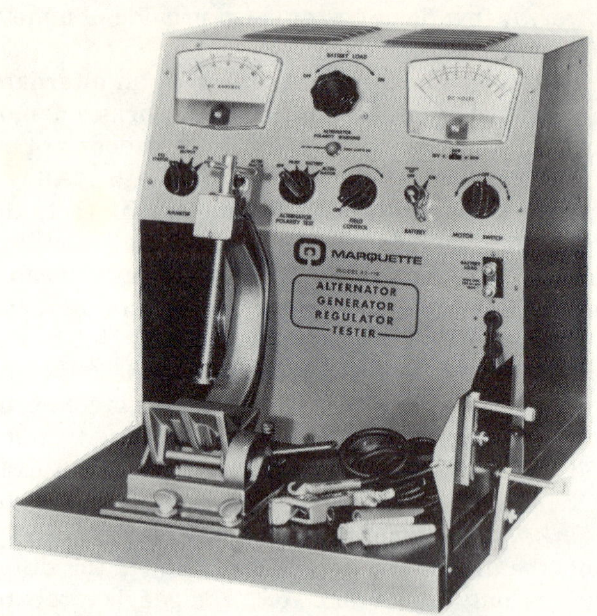

Courtesy Marquette Mfg. Co.

Fig. 5-6. A bench-type alternator tester which will also check generators and regulators.

Courtesy Sun Electric Corp.

Fig. 5-7. A large floor-model alternator tester.

various tests discussed in the beginning of this chapter. However, by properly interpreting the test results, you can usually narrow down the most likely causes of the trouble.

For example, if the alternator produces no output current at all, the problem may be an open wye connection or possibly an open field circuit. Most bench testers have a field-current ammeter which would quickly show if the field were open (field current would be zero in this case). The next step would be to confirm it with an ohmmeter check of the field coil. In another instance, the output current may be only about half of what is specified. A logical assumption in this situation would be a shorted diode. Some bench testers have a circuit specifically designed to detect faulty diodes. However, you would still have to disassemble the alternator and make individual diode checks to locate the offending component.

The instrument in Fig. 5-6 offers considerable testing flexibility. Among the various controls are a variable carbon pile for simulating a full range of electrical loads, a field-current rheostat to control the amount of field current for precise output tests, a multirange ammeter and voltmeter, and a motor-reversing switch. The last item is primarily used when testing generators, which, of course, must be rotated in the proper direction. In addition, regulators can also be checked on this tester. An even more elaborate bench tester is shown in Fig. 5-7.

Bench testers, such as those just shown, are very desirable instruments to have and are a great convenience for shops that specialize in charging-system work. However, as we have said before, they are not an absolute necessity, especially if you do not have the volume of work to justify them. You can still do an acceptable job of alternator bench repair using the instruments and procedures previously described. The worst that can happen is that you may incorrectly diagnose a problem and have to remove the alternator a second time. The important thing to remember is that alternators are not the mysterious devices you may have been led to believe. There are only a relatively few things to go wrong and these are easily spotted with the proper instruments and procedures.

CHAPTER 6

Delco-Remy Charging Systems

TWO-UNIT REGULATORS

These regulators feature a double-contact voltage regulator unit and slip-on type connector terminals. The wiring harness connector is easily detached from the regulator by lifting the latch which clears a projection on the harness connector. See Fig. 6-1.

To avoid damage to the electrical equipment, always observe the following precautions.

1. Do not polarize the generator.
2. Do not short across or ground any of the terminals in the charging circuit except as specifically instructed.
3. *Never* operate the generator with the output terminal open-circuited and the field circuit energized.
4. Make sure the generator, regulator, and battery have the same ground polarity.
5. When connecting a charger or a booster battery to the vehicle battery, connect negative to negative and positive to positive.

Operating Principles

A typical circuit diagram for the two-unit regulator is shown in Fig. 6-2. Following is a brief description of the operating principles of this type of circuit using an indicator lamp. The same general principles apply when an ammeter is used.

When the ignition switch is closed, before the engine has started, the indicator lamp lights to indicate the generator is not charging. The current flow can be traced from the battery to the BAT terminal on the switch, through the indicator lamp and resistor which are in parallel, and then through the closed voltage-regulator contacts. From here it continues to flow on through the generator field winding to ground, completing the circuit back to the battery. Current through this circuit energizes the field windings sufficiently to ensure voltage buildup in the stator windings when the engine starts. The voltages generated in the stator windings are then changed or rectified by the six generator diodes to a dc voltage which appears at the BAT or output terminal on the generator. The resistor in parallel with the lamp allows more current to flow through the field winding to ensure voltage buildup in the stator windings.

As the generator begins to operate, voltage from the "R" or relay terminal on the generator is impressed through regulator terminal No. 2 across the field relay winding, causing the relay contacts to close. This connects regulator terminal No. 4 directly to the battery through the field relay contacts, causing the indicator lamp to go out. Gen-

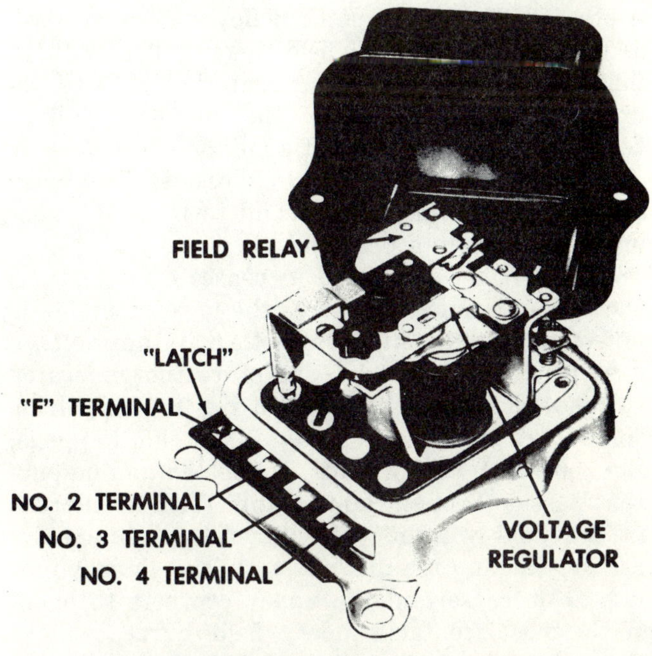

Fig. 6-1. Delco-Remy two-unit regulator.

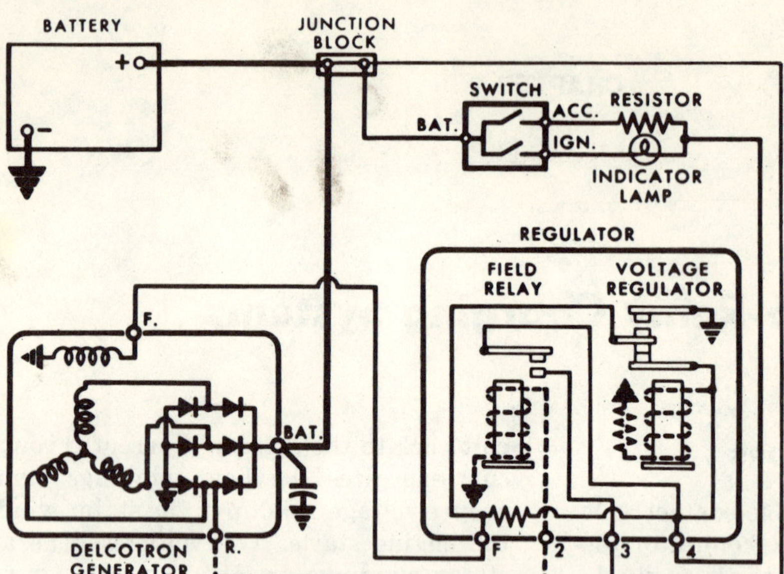

Fig. 6-2. Circuit diagram for two-unit voltage regulator.

erator field current then flows from the battery to regulator terminal No. 3, and then through the field relay contacts and the lower or series contacts of the voltage regulator to the field winding.

As the speed of the generator increases, the voltage at the BAT terminal of the generator also increases. This impresses a higher voltage through the field relay contacts and across the voltage-regulator shunt winding. The increased magnetism created by this higher voltage across the winding causes the lower contacts of the regulator to separate. The field current then flows through a resistor which reduces the field current. This reduced field current causes the generator voltage to decrease, thereby decreasing the magnetic pull of the voltage-regulator shunt winding. Consequently the spring causes the contacts to reclose. This cycle repeats many times per second to limit the generator voltage to a preset value.

As the generator speed increases even further, the resistor connected across the lower contacts is not of sufficiently high value to maintain voltage control on the contacts. Therefore the generator voltage increases slightly causing the upper or "shorting" contacts to close. When this happens, the generator field winding is shorted and no current passes through the winding. With no current in the field winding, the generator voltage decreases causing the magnetism in the shunt winding to decrease and the upper contacts to open. With these contacts open, field current flows through the resistor and the field winding. As the voltage increases, the upper contacts reclose. This cycle then repeats many times per second to limit the generator voltage to a preset value at high generator speeds. The voltage-regulator unit thus operates to limit the value of generator voltage throughout the generator speed range. Consequently the electrical accessories are protected from excessive voltage which would cause damage to them.

Troubleshooting Procedures

Close adherence to the following procedures in the order presented will lead to the location and correction of charging-system defects in the shortest possible time. It will not be necessary to perform all of these procedures in order to locate the trouble.

A wiring diagram showing basic lead connections to the regulator is shown in Fig. 6-3. Note that an ammeter may be used in this circuit without an indicator lamp. In this case, condition A listed below pertaining to the indicator lamp does not apply.

Trouble in the charging system usually will show up as one or more of the following three major conditions.

A. Faulty indicator lamp operation.
B. An undercharged battery as evidenced by slow cranking.
C. An overcharged battery as evidenced by excessive water usage.

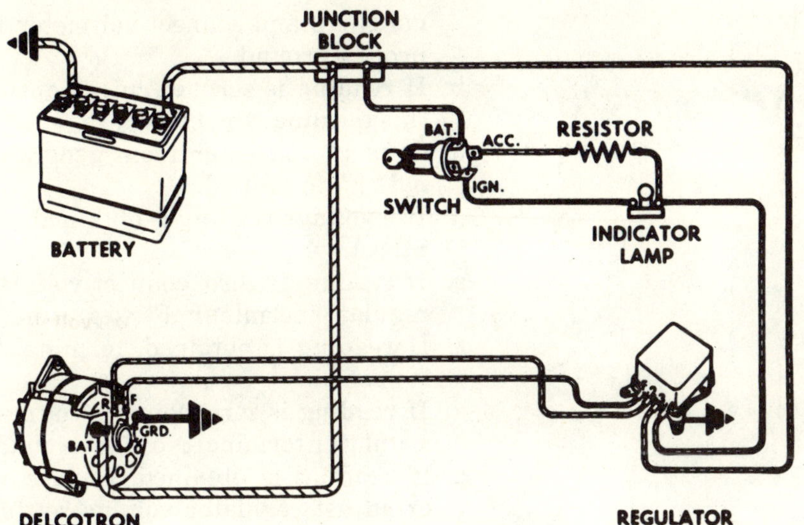

Fig. 6-3. Basic wiring diagram for complete charging system.

A. Faulty Indicator Lamp Operation

Check the indicator lamp for normal operation as shown below.

SWITCH	LAMP	ENGINE
Off	*Off*	*Stopped*
On	*On*	*Stopped*
On	*Off*	*Idling*

If the indicator lamp operates normally, follow the procedures listed under *Undercharged Battery* or *Overcharged Battery.* Otherwise, inspect all connections including the slip-on type connectors at the generator, regulator, and firewall for poor connections. Check the wiring harness for grounds. If everything checks satisfactorily, or if this troubleshooting procedure does not correct the problem, proceed to *either one* of the following three *abnormal* conditions.

1. Switch Off, Lamp On—In this case check for a shorted diode in the generator according to the applicable generator service bulletin. This condition will cause a discharged battery. If the generator does not have a shorted diode, check for a short between leads terminals Nos. 2, 3, and 4 at the regulator.
2. Switch on, Lamp Off, Engine Stopped—The only cause of this condition is an open in the indicator lamp circuit. Check as follows with ignition switch on.

   a. Detach harness connector from regulator and connect jumper as shown in Fig. 6-4.
   b. If lamp does not light, check for a blown fuse, a burned-out bulb, defective bulb socket, or an open lead in circuit between regulator terminal No. 4 and ignition switch.
   c. If lamp lights, connect jumper lead as shown in Fig. 6-5.
   d. If lamp lights, replace regulator or adjust regulator voltage setting.
   e. If lamp does not light, leave jumper as shown in Fig. 6-5, connect second jumper from generator terminal "F" to ground.
   f. If lamp does not light, terminal "F" lead is open circuited.
   g. If lamp lights, generator field is open cir-

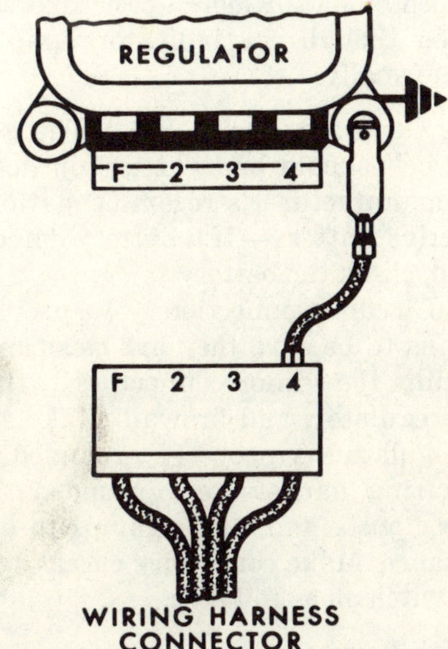

Fig. 6-4. Checking the indicator lamp circuit, step 1.

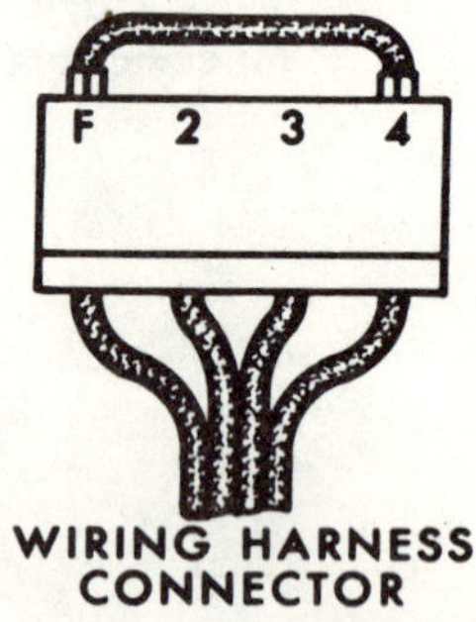

Fig. 6-5. Checking the indicator lamp circuit, step 2.

cuited; repair according to the applicable generator service bulletin.

3. Switch On, Lamp On, Engine Idling—The possible causes of this condition are covered in Steps 1, 3, 4, 5, and 6 under *Undercharged Battery.*

If the defect has been found and corrected at this point, no further checks need be made.

B. Undercharged Battery

This condition, as evidenced by slow cranking, can be caused by one or more of the following conditions even though the indicator lamp may be operating normally.

1. Loose Generator Drive Belt—The generator drive belt should be tightened in accordance with manufacturer's recommendations.
2. Defective Battery—If a battery defect is suspected, check the battery.
3. Poor Circuit Connections—Inspect all connections to be sure they are clean and tight, including the slip-on connectors at the generator, regulator, and firewall. Make sure that the regulator is properly grounded. Inspect the wiring harness for grounds. Clean the battery posts and cable clamps to eliminate resistance. Make continuity checks with ignition switch on as follows:
   a. With harness connector attached to regulator, slide test prod into regulator terminal No. 3 and connect voltmeter from test prod to ground.
   b. If reading is zero, circuit is open between this terminal and battery.
   c. Connect voltmeter from generator terminal "F" to ground.
   d. If a voltage reading is obtained, proceed to Step 4.
   e. If reading is zero, connect voltmeter from regulator terminal "F" to ground.
   f. If reading is obtained, terminal "F" lead is open.
   g. If reading is zero, connect voltmeter from regulator terminal No. 4 to ground.
   h. If reading is obtained, replace regulator or adjust regulator voltage setting.
   i. If reading is zero, circuit is open between terminal No. 4 and ignition switch.
4. An Open Resistor—Connector voltmeter from regulator terminal No. 4 to ground. Turn ignition switch to ACC position. If reading is zero, resistor connected to ACC terminal is open.
5. Malfunction of Field Relay—If the indicator lamp operates normally, it is not necessary to check the field relay; go to Step 6. However, if the indicator lamp fails to go out with the generator in operation, or the ammeter fails to function normally in circuits using an ammeter, check the field relay as follows:
   a. Connect a voltmeter from regulator terminal No. 2.
   b. Operate engine slightly above idle speed.
   c. If voltmeter reads 5 volts or more, and the *indicator lamp fails to go out,* replace regulator.

      For *ammeter* circuits, if reading is 5 volts or more, connect voltmeter from regulator terminal No. 3 to regulator terminal No. 4. If reading is over 1 volt, replace regulator.
   d. If reading is below 5 volts, connect voltmeter from generator terminal "R" to ground.
   e. If reading now is 5 volts or more, the lead between generator terminal "R" and regulator terminal No. 2 is defective.
   f. If reading is still below 5 volts, proceed to Step 6.
6. Defective Generator—To determine if the

generator is operating properly, proceed as follows:

a. Disconnect battery ground strap.
b. Connect an ammeter in series with the circuit at the BAT terminal of the generator and a voltmeter from the BAT terminal to ground.
c. Connect a jumper lead to the harness connector as shown in Fig. 6-6.
d. Reconnect battery ground strap.
e. Turn lights on high beam and blower motor on high speed.
f. Operate engine at 1500-2500 rpm as required to obtain maximum current output. CAUTION: If voltage exceeds 16 volts, connect a carbon-pile load across battery to keep voltage below 16 volts.
g. If current output is within 10 amperes of rated output as stamped on generator frame, generator is good. Otherwise, repair generator according to the applicable generator service bulletin.
h. An *alternate* method of checking generator output is to make connections as outlined above, operate at specified speed, and compare output with data in Delco-Remy Specification Bulletins 1G-186 or 1G-187. Output may vary slightly depending on generator temperature.
i. Turn lights and blower off. Remove jumper lead from harness connector.

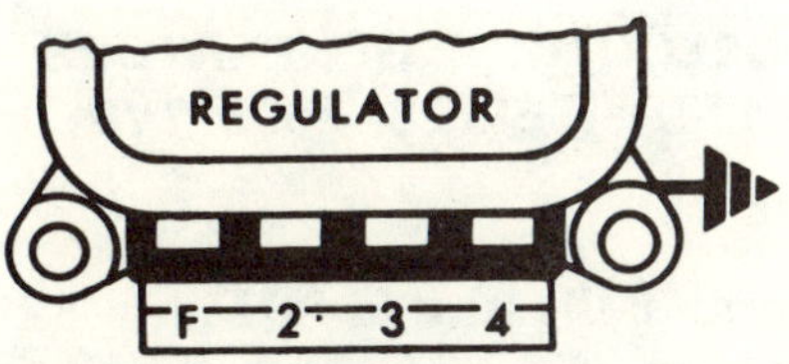

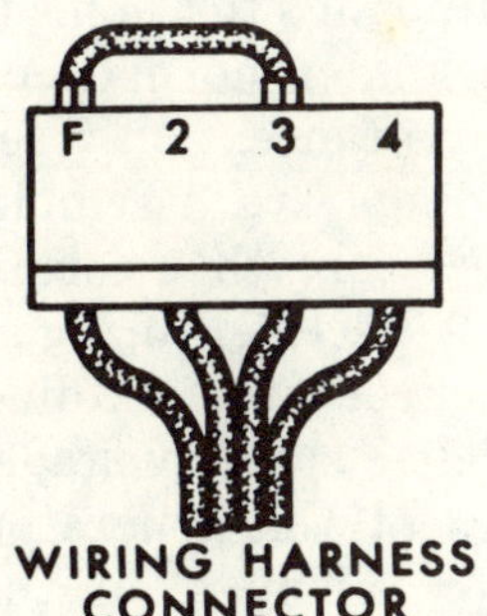

Fig. 6-6. Jumper connection for checking generator output.

7. Low-Voltage Regulator Setting—If no reason for the discharged battery condition has been found by the preceding checks, refer to the following section entitled *Adjusting The Voltage Setting.*

C. Overcharged Battery

An overcharged battery, as evidenced by excessive water usage, can be caused by:

1. Defective Battery—If a defective battery is suspected, check by any standard method.
2. Poor Circuit Connections—Inspect all connections to make sure they are clean and tight, particularly the circuit between the battery and regulator terminal No. 3. Also, check the regulator ground connection.
3. High-Voltage Regulator Setting—If no circuit defects are found, yet the battery remains overcharged, proceed to the following section entitled *Adjusting The Voltage Setting.*

Adjusting the Voltage Setting

It is important to remember that the voltage setting for one type of operating condition may not be satisfactory for another type of operating condition. The proper setting is attained when the battery remains fully charged with a minimum use of water.

The voltage at which the regulator operates varies with changes in regulator ambient temperatures. The ambient temperature is the temperature of the air measured ¼ inch from the regulator cover. When checking and adjusting the voltage setting, always refer to the manufacturer's specifications.

To check and adjust the voltage setting, proceed as follows:

1. Insert a test prod into regulator terminal No. 3, and connect a voltmeter from test prod to ground.
2. Disconnect cable at the negative battery post and insert ¼-ohm, 25-watt resistor in series with it. NOTE: If battery is sufficiently charged to limit generator output to 10 amperes or less when adjusting voltage setting, the ¼-ohm resistor need not be used.
3. Short across resistor with jumper cable, start engine, and then remove jumper cable. Do not operate with battery disconnected.

4. With all accessories turned off and wiring harness connected to regulator, operate engine at idle speed for 15 minutes to establish regulator operating temperature.
5. Cycle the regulator by detaching then reconnecting the wiring harness connector at the regulator, or by stopping then restarting the engine.
6. Bring engine speed up to 2000-2200 rpm, note ambient temperature and voltage setting. Compare with manufacturer's specifications.
7. To adjust voltage setting:
   a. Detach regulator wiring harness connector, remove cover, and then reconnect wiring harness connector.
   b. Turn *adjusting screw* as shown in Fig. 6-7.
   c. For undercharged battery, raise voltage setting to upper part of specification range.
   d. For overcharged battery, lower voltage setting to lower part of specification range.
   e. *CAUTION*: Make sure that springholder is against head of screw. When turning adjusting screw counterclockwise, turn until screwhead is about ⅛ inch above holder, pry holder up against screwhead, and then turn *clockwise* to make *final* setting.
8. After making the final setting, cycle the regulator according to preceding Step 5.
9. Then operate engine at 2000-2200 rpm and note voltage setting. Readjust voltage if necessary. Always cycle (Step 8) before reading final voltage setting.
10. This procedure has adjusted the voltage setting while operating the regulator on the upper or shorting contacts. Now proceed to adjust the voltage setting on the lower or series contacts as follows.
11. Turn on parking lights, slowly *decrease* engine speed from the 2000-2200 rpm value and observe voltmeter. When operation changes from upper to lower contacts, voltmeter reading should suddenly decrease a few tenths of a volt. (See manufacturer's specifications. Compare difference in voltage readings with specifications.)
12. To decrease the difference in voltage between upper and lower contact operation, turn the nylon nut (Fig. 6-7) slightly clockwise. To increase the difference, turn nylon nut counterclockwise. If this adjustment is made, the voltage setting must be rechecked as covered in Steps 5 through 11.

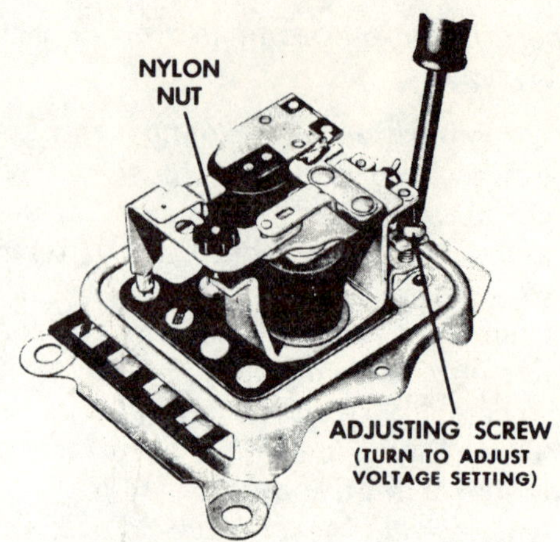

Fig. 6-7. Adjusting the voltage setting.

13. If voltage-regulator operation is erratic, and if the regulator cannot be adjusted to a steady value, replace the regulator and check the generator field winding for shorts. *Do not attempt to clean the contact points.*
14. *IMPORTANT*: Always remove wiring harness connector at regulator when removing or replacing cover to avoid accidental grounds and consequent damage to regulator.

DELCOTRON GENERATORS 10-DN SERIES, 100B TYPE

Introduction

The generator illustrated in Fig. 6-8 contains a sufficient supply of lubricant to eliminate the need for periodic lubrication. The brushes carry current through the two slip rings to the field coil mounted on the rotor, and, under normal conditions, will provide long periods of attention-free service.

The stator windings are assembled on the inside of a laminated core that forms part of the generator frame. A rectifier bridge connected to the stator windings contains six diodes, and electrically changes the ac stator voltage to a dc voltage which appears at the generator output terminal. A capacitor mounted in the end frame protects the rectifier bridge from high voltages and suppresses radio noise.

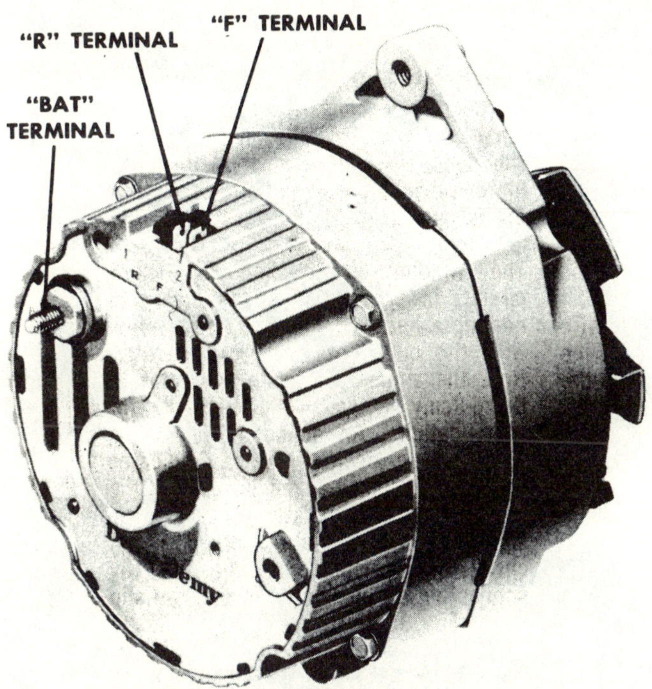

Fig. 6-8. Externally regulated Delcotron generator (10-DN Series, 100B Type).

No periodic adjustments or maintenance of any kind are required for the entire generator assembly. An internal wiring circuit is shown in Fig. 6-9.

To avoid damage when working on the charging circuit, observe the following precautions:

1. Do not polarize the generator.
2. Do not short across or ground any of the terminals in the charging circuit except as specifically instructed herein.
3. *Never* operate the generator with the output terminal open-circuited.
4. Make sure the generator and battery have the same polarity.
5. When connecting a charger or a booster battery to the vehicle battery connect negative to negative and positive to positive.

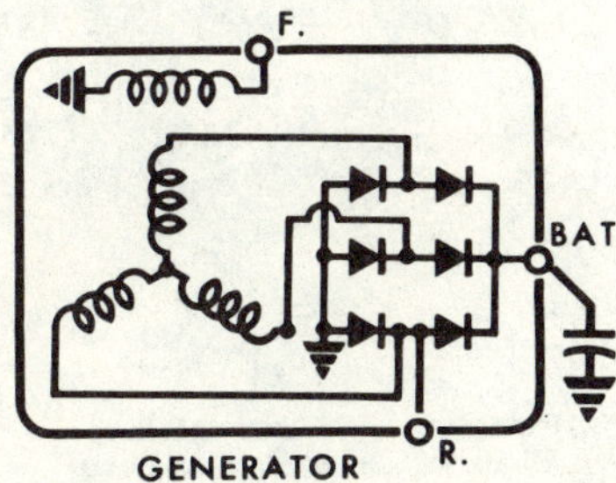

Fig. 6-9. Typical wiring diagram for the Delcotron generator.

Noisy Generator

Noise from the generator may be caused by worn or dirty bearings, loose mounting bolts, broken end frames, a loose drive pulley, a defective diode in the rectifier bridge, or a defective stator.

Disassembly

To disassemble the generator, take out the four thru-bolts and separate the drive end frame and rotor assembly from the stator assembly by prying apart with a screwdriver at the stator slot. A scribe mark will help locate the parts in the same position during reassembly. After disassembly, place a piece of tape over the slip-ring end frame bearing to prevent entry of dirt and other foreign material, and also place a piece of tape over the shaft on slip-ring end. *CAUTION:* Use pressure-sensitive tape and not friction tape which would leave a gummy deposit on the shaft. If brushes are to be reused, clean with a soft, dry cloth.

To remove the drive end frame from the rotor, place the rotor in a vise and tighten only enough to permit removal of the shaft nut. *CAUTION:* Avoid excessive tightening as this may cause distortion of the rotor. Remove the shaft, nut, washer, pulley, fan, and the collar, and then separate the drive end frame from the rotor shaft.

Rotor-Field Winding Checks

To check for opens, connect a test lamp or an ohmmeter to each slip ring. If the lamp fails to light, or if the ohmmeter reading is high (infinite), the winding is open (Fig. 6-10).

The winding is checked for short circuits or excessive resistance by connecting a battery and ammeter in series with the edges of the two slip rings. Note the ammeter reading and refer to Delco-Remy Service Bulletin 1G-187 for specifications. An ammeter reading above the specified value indicates shorted windings; a reading below the specified value indicates excessive resistance. An alternate method is to check the resistance of the field by connecting an ohmmeter to the two slip rings (Fig. 6-10). If the resistance reading is below the specified value, the winding is shorted; if it is above the specified value, the winding has excessive resistance. The specified resistance can be determined by dividing the voltage by the current given in bulletin 1G-187. Remember that the winding resistance and ammeter readings will vary slightly with winding temperature changes. If the

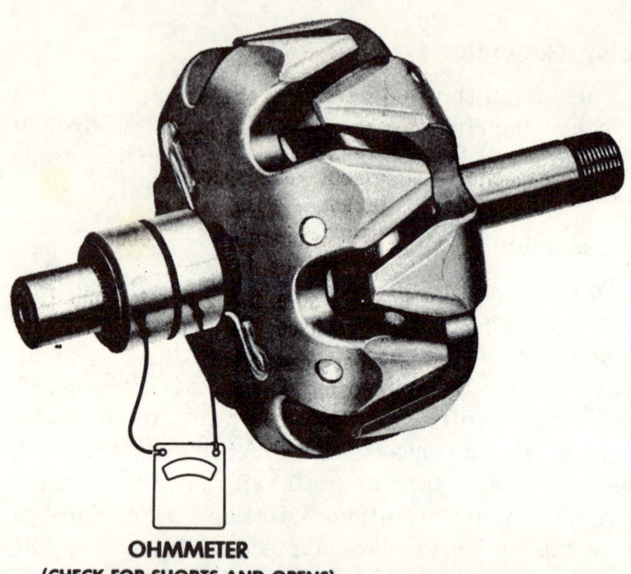

Fig. 6-10. Checking the rotor winding for continuity.

rotor is not defective, but the generator fails to supply rated output, the defect is in the rectifier bridge or stator.

Rectifier Bridge Check

Note that the rectifier bridge has a grounded heat sink and an insulated heat sink connected to the output terminal. Also, note the insulating washer located between the insulated heat sink and the end frame.

To check the rectifier bridge, remove the stator and then connect the ohmmeter to the grounded heat sink and to one of the three flat metal clips (Fig. 6-11). Press down firmly on the clip. *Do not connect to threaded stud.*

Then reverse the lead connections to the grounded heat sink and the same flat metal clip. If both readings are the same, replace the rectifier bridge. A good rectifier bridge will give a high reading in one direction and a low reading in the other. Repeat this same test between the grounded heat sink and the other two clips. Also, make this test between the insulated heat sink and each of the three clips. This makes a total of six checks, with two readings taken for each check.

The ohmmeter check of the rectifier bridge is a valid and accurate check. *Do not replace the rectifier bridge* unless at least one pair of readings is the same. CAUTION: Do not use high voltage to check these units, such as a 110-volt test lamp.

To replace the rectifier bridge, remove the attaching screws and disconnect the capacitor lead.

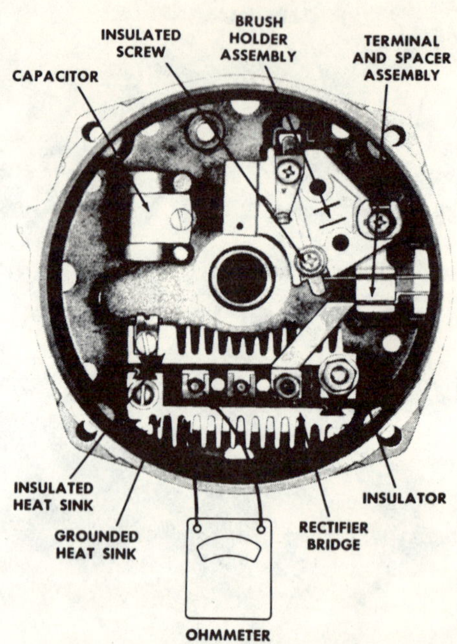

Fig. 6-11. Checking the rectifier bridge.

Note the insulator between the insulated heat sink and end frame (Fig. 6-11). Rectifier bridges may vary in appearance but are completely interchangeable in these generators.

Stator Winding Checks

The stator windings may be checked with a 110-volt test lamp or an ohmmeter. If the lamp lights or the ohmmeter reading is low when connected from any stator lead to the frame, the windings are grounded. If the lamp fails to light or the readings are high when connected between successive pairs of stator leads, the windings are open (Fig. 6-12).

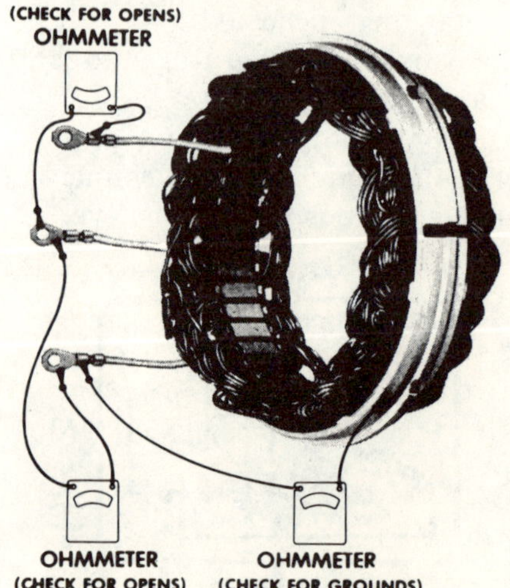

Fig. 6-12. Checking the stator winding.

A short circuit in the stator windings is difficult to locate without laboratory test equipment due to the low resistance of the windings. However, if all other electrical checks are normal, and the generator fails to supply rated output, shorted stator windings are indicated. Also, a shorted stator winding can cause the charging-system indicator lamp to come on with the engine at a low speed.

Brush Holder Replacement

Remove the three screws to replace the brush holder assembly, noting carefully the location of the insulated screw (Fig. 6-11).

Slip-Ring Servicing

If the slip rings are dirty, they may be cleaned and finished with 400-grain or finer polishing cloth. Spin the rotor and hold the polishing cloth against the slip rings until they are clean. *CAUTION:* The rotor must be rotated in order that the slip rings will be cleaned evenly. Cleaning the slip rings by hand, without spinning the rotor, may result in flat spots on the slip rings which can cause brush noise.

Slip rings which are rough or out-of-round should be trued in a lathe to .002-inch maximum indicator reading. Remove only enough material to make the rings smooth and round. Finish with 400-grain polishing cloth and blow away all dust.

Bearing Replacement and Lubrication

The bearing in the drive end frame can be removed by detaching the retainer plate screws and then pressing the bearing from the end frame. If the bearing is in satisfactory condition, it may be reused. Refill one-quarter full with Delco-Remy lubricant No. 1948791 before reassembly. *CAUTION:* Do not overfill as this may cause the bearing to overheat; use only the specified lubricant.

To install a new bearing, press in with a tube or collar that just fits over the outer race. It is recommended that a new retainer plate be installed if the felt seal in the retainer plate is hardened or excessively worn. Fill the cavity between the retainer plate and the bearing with 1948791 lubricant.

The bearing in the slip-ring end frame should be replaced if its grease supply is exhausted. No attempt should be made to relubricate or reuse the bearing. To remove the bearing from the slip-ring end frame, press out with a tube or collar that just fits the inside of the end-frame housing. Press from the outside of the housing toward the inside.

To install a new bearing, place a flat plate over the bearing and press in from the outside until the bearing is flush with the outside of the frame. Support the inside of the frame with a hollow cylinder to prevent breakage of the end frame. Use extreme care to avoid misalignment or undue stress on the bearing. Lightly coat the seal lip with oil to facilitate assembly of the shaft into the bearing.

Reassembly

Reassembly is the reverse of disassembly. When installing the pulley, remember to secure the rotor in a vise only tight enough to permit tightening the shaft nut to 40-60 lb. ft. If excessive pressure is applied against the rotor, the assembly may become distorted. To install the slip-ring end frame assembly to the rotor and the drive end frame assembly, remove the tape over the bearing and shaft and make sure the shaft is perfectly clean after removing the tape. Insert a pin through the holes to hold up the brushes. Carefully install the shaft into the slip-ring end frame to avoid damaging the seal. After tightening the thru-bolts, remove the brush retaining pin to allow the brushes to contact the slip rings.

Generator Bench Check

To check the generator in a test stand, proceed as follows:

1. Make connections as shown in Fig. 6-13. Connect negative battery post to generator frame on negative-ground units.
2. Set speed and carbon pile as required to obtain maximum current at rated voltage. See Bulletin 1G-187.
3. Generator is good if output is within 10 percent of output stamped on frame. If not, repair as described in the preceding sections.

DELCOTRON GENERATORS 10-SI AND 27-SI SERIES, 100 TYPE

Introduction

The Delcotron generators illustrated in Figs. 6-14, 6-15, and 6-16 feature a solid-state regulator mounted inside the slip-ring end frame. All regulator components are installed in a solid mold and, along with the brush-holder assembly, attached to the slip-ring end frame. The regulator voltage setting never needs adjusting and no provision is made for this.

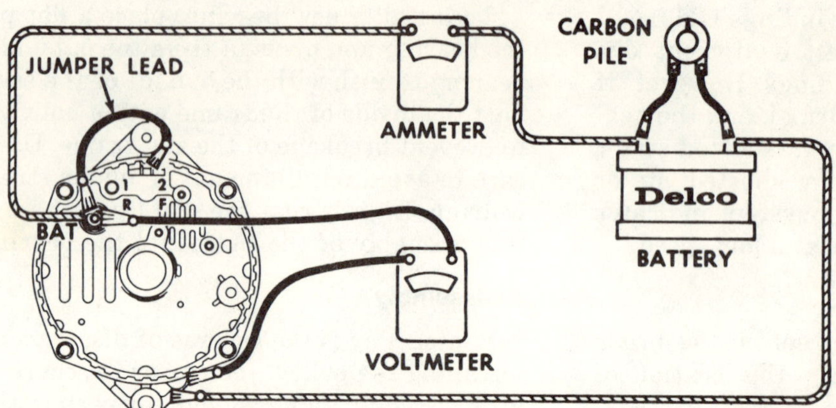

Fig. 6-13. Checking generator output.

The bearings do not require periodic lubrication as they contain a sufficient supply of lubricant. The brushes carry current through the slip rings to the field coil in the rotor and, under normal conditions, provide attention-free service over long periods.

The stator windings are assembled on the inside of a laminated core that forms part of the generator frame. A rectifier bridge connected to the stator windings contains six diodes. These change the ac stator voltage to the dc voltage that appears at the generator output terminal. Generator field current is supplied through a diode trio, which also is connected to the stator windings. A capacitor mounted in the end frame protects the rectifier bridge and diode trio from high voltages and also suppresses radio noise.

No periodic adjustments or maintenance of any kind are required on the entire generator assembly.

Operating Principles

A typical 10-SI Series wiring diagram is shown in Fig. 6-17. The 27-SI Series is the same except the stator is delta connected. The basic operating principles are as follows.

When the switch is closed, current from the battery flows through the indicator lamp and resistor to the generator terminal No. 1, through resistor R1, diode D1, and the base-emitter junction

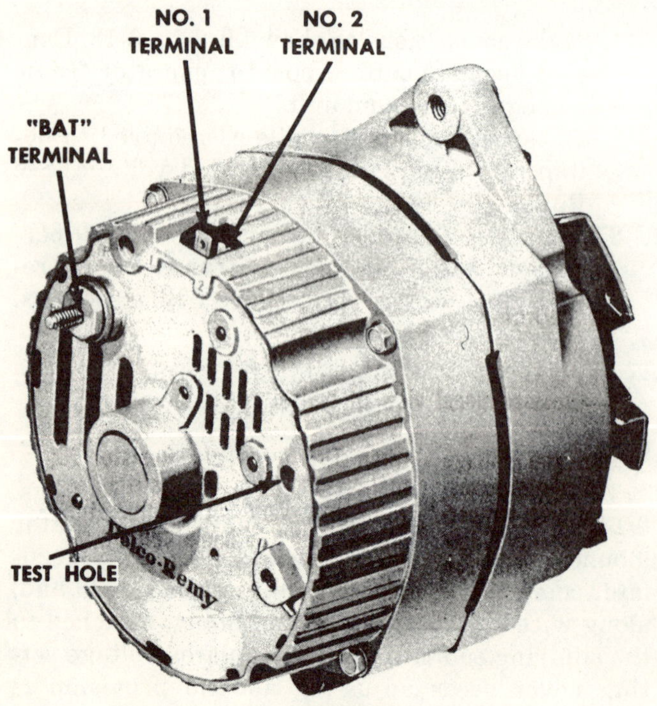

Fig. 6-14. 10-SI Series Delcotron generator.

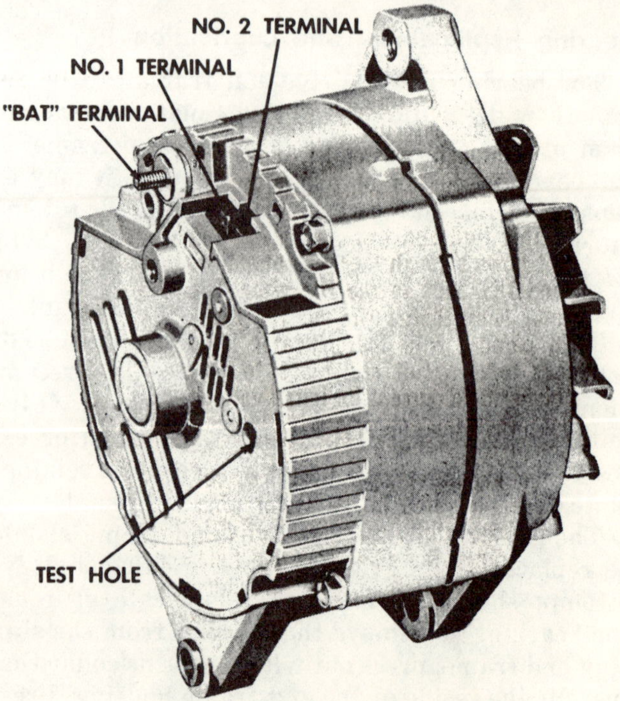

Fig. 6-15. 27-SI Series Delcotron generator.

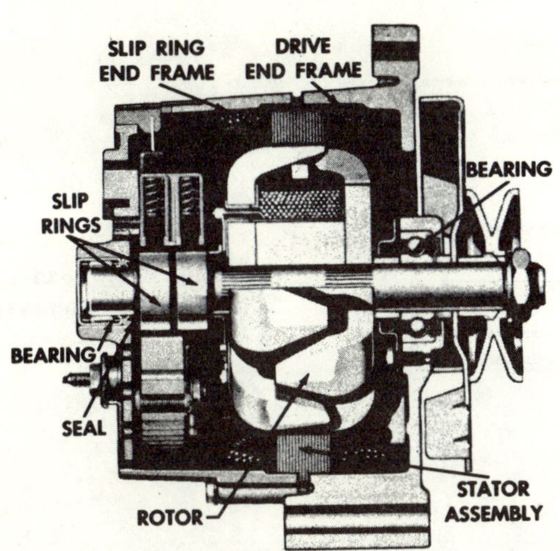

Fig. 6-16. Cross-sectional view of Delcotron generator.

of transistor TR1 to ground and then back to the battery. This turns on transistor TR1 allowing current to flow through the field coil (rotor), TR1, and back to the battery. The indicator lamp then turns on. The resistor in parallel with the indicator lamp allows sufficiently high field current for initial voltage buildup when the engine starts.

With the rotor turning and current flowing through its coil, ac voltages are generated in the stator windings. The stator also supplies ac voltage to the diode trio which rectifies it to dc in order to supply field current to the rotor. The flow of this field current is controlled by the regulator. The six diodes in the rectifier bridge convert the ac voltage of the stator windings into the dc voltage that appears between the generator BAT terminal and ground. As generator speed increase, current is provided for charging the battery and supplying the various electrical accessories. This charging current also causes the same voltage to appear both the BAT terminal and at terminal No. 1. With no voltage difference across the lamp, it goes out, indicating that the generator is producing an output.

Although terminal No. 2 is permanently connected to the battery, the discharge current is negligible because of the high resistances of R2 and R3. As generator voltage increases, the voltage between R2 and R3 likewise increase. At a preadjusted point, this voltage is sufficient to cause zener diode D2 to conduct. This turns on transistor TR2 which then turns *off* TR1, stopping the flow of field current. With field current off, the generator voltage decreases. Now, diode D2 stops conducting, transistor TR 2 turns off and transistor

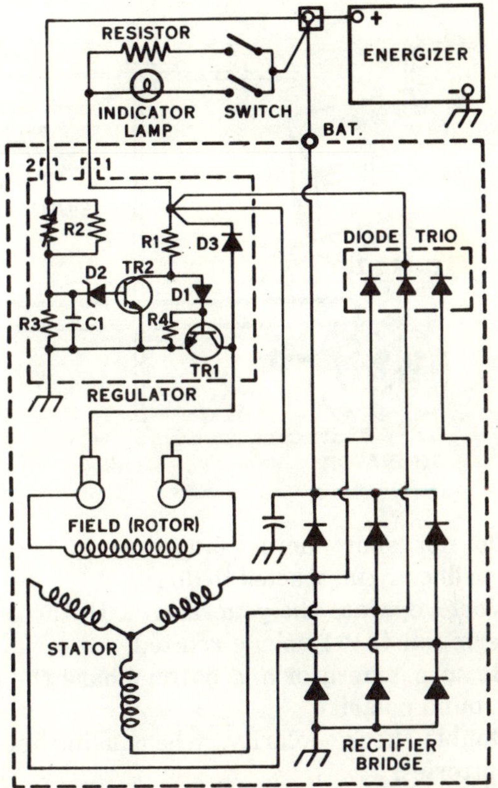

Fig. 6-17. Wiring diagram for Delcotron 10-SI Series generator.

TR1 turns *on*. Field current once again flows and the whole process repeats itself. The generator goes through many of these cycles each second which, in effect, limits the generator voltage to a preset value—the regulated voltage.

Capacitor C1 smooths out the voltage across resistor R3. Resistor R4 prevents excess current through transistor TR1 at high temperatures and diode D3 prevents high induced voltages in the field windings when TR1 turns off. Resistor R2 is shunted with a thermistor which causes the regulated voltage to vary with the temperature and thus, provides the optimum voltage for charging the battery.

Troubleshooting Procedures

Following these procedures in the order given will enable you to locate the problem in the shortest possible time. Only a portion of these procedures need be followed to pinpoint a specific problem.

Fig. 6-18 is a basic wiring diagram showing lead connections for the charging system. To avoid damage, always observe the following precautions:

1. Do not polarize the generator.

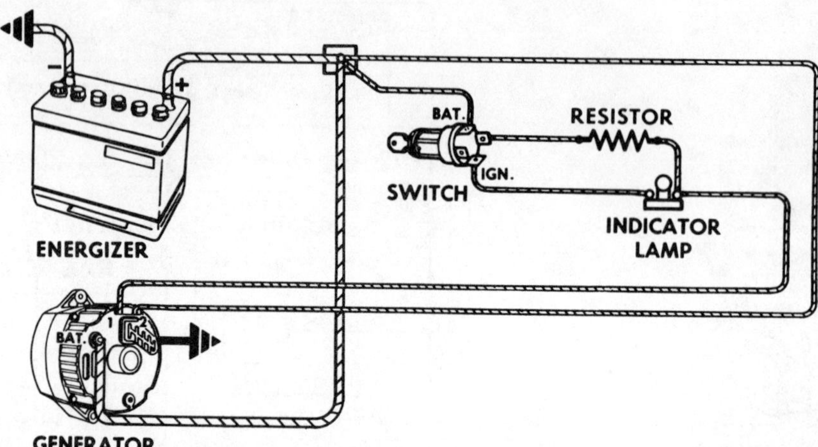

Fig. 6-18. Basic lead connections for charging system.

2. Do not short across any terminals unless specifically instructed to do so.
3. *Never* operate the generator with the output terminal (BAT) open-circuited.
4. Be sure generator and battery have the same ground polarity.
5. Double-check polarity when using booster batteries.

NOTE: In some circuits an ammeter may be used instead of an indicator lamp. In these cases, condition A which pertains to the indicator lamp should be omitted.

Trouble in the charging system will show up as one or more of the following conditions:

A. Faulty indicator lamp operation.
B. An undercharged battery as evidenced by a hydrometer test or other battery test procedure or by a slow-cranking starter.
C. An overcharged battery as indicated by excessive water usage.

A. Faulty Indicator Lamp Operation

Check the lamp for normal operation as shown below.

SWITCH	LAMP	ENGINE
Off	*Off*	*Stopped*
On	*On*	*Stopped*
On	*Off*	*Running*

If the indicator lamp operates normally, proceed to *Undercharged Battery* section. Otherwise, proceed to either *one* of the following three *abnormal* conditions.

1. Switch Off, Lamp On—In this case, disconnect the two leads from generator terminals No. 1 and 2. If the lamp stays on, there is a short between these two leads. If the lamp goes out, replace the rectifier bridge as covered in the *Generator Repair* section. This condition will cause an undercharged battery.
2. Switch On, Lamp Off, Engine Stopped—This condition can be caused by the defects listed for Condition 1 above, by the reversal of leads at generator terminals No. 1 and 2, or by an open in the circuit. This condition can cause an undercharged battery. To determine where an open exists, proceed as follows:

a. Connect voltmeter from generator terminal No. 2 to ground. If a reading is obtained, go to Step b. If reading is zero, repair open circuit between terminal No. 2 and battery. Indicator lamp should now come on; if so, no further checks need be made.
b. With ignition on, disconnect lead No. 1 from generator and ground it. CAUTION: Never ground lead No. 2.
c. If lamp does not light, check for a blown fuse, a burned-out bulb, a defective bulb socket, or an open lead between generator terminal No. 1 and the ignition switch.
d. If lamp lights, unground lead No. 1 and reconnect to generator. Insert screwdriver into test hole (Fig. 6-19) to ground field winding.
e. If lamp does not light, check connections between wiring harness and terminal No. 1. Also check the brushes, slip ring, and

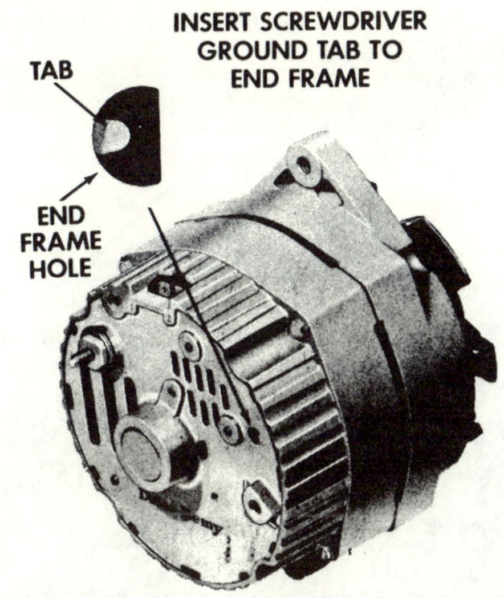

Fig. 6-19. Grounding generator field winding to make output tests.

field winding for opens as covered in *Generator Repair* section.

f. If lamp lights and a voltmeter reading was obtained in Step a, replace the regulator as covered in the *Generator Repair* section.

3. Switch On, Lamp On, Engine Running—Check for a blown fuse (when used) between indicator lamp and switch. The other possible causes of this condition are covered in the *Undercharged Battery* section. If a defect has been found and corrected at this point, no further check need be made.

B. Undercharged Battery

This condition, as evidenced by slow cranking and low specific gravity, can be caused by one or more of the following conditions, even though the indicator lamp may be operating normally. The following procedure also applies to circuits using an ammeter.

1. Make sure the undercharged condition has not been caused by accessories being inadvertently left on.
2. Check drive belt for proper tension.
3. Check for battery defects using an acceptable battery tester.
4. Inspect for wiring defects and check all connections, battery cables, and clamps for tightness and cleanliness.
5. With ignition on and all wiring connected, connect a voltmeter from:

a. Generator BAT terminal to ground.
b. Generator terminal No. 1 to ground.
c. Generator terminal No. 2 to ground.

A zero reading on any of the above three checks indicates an open circuit between the affected terminal and the battery. NOTE: An open No. 2 lead on early production units caused uncontrolled voltage, resulting in battery overcharge and possible damage to accessories. Later production units have a built-in feature that prevents the generator from producing an output if this lead is open.

6. If Steps 1 through 5 show satisfactory results, check the generator as follows:

a. Disconnect battery ground cable.
b. Connect a test ammeter in series with the circuit at the BAT terminal of the generator.
c. Reconnect the ground cable.
d. Turn on radio, windshield wipers, high-beam headlights, and blower motor (high speed). Connect a carbon pile across the battery.
e. Operate engine at moderate speed and adjust carbon pile to obtain maximum output.
f. If current output is within 10 percent of the rated output as stamped on the generator frame, the generator is not defective. Recheck Steps 1 through 5.
g. If output is not within 10 percent of rated output, ground the field winding by inserting a screwdriver into the test hole to ground tab shown in Fig. 6-19. CAUTION: Tab is within ¾ inch of the casting surface. Do not force screwdriver deeper than one inch.
h. With screwdriver grounding the tab and the engine operating at moderate speed, note ammeter reading.
i. If output is now within 10 percent of rated output, replace regulator as covered in *Generator Repair* section. Also, check field winding.
j. If output still is not within 10 percent, check field winding, diode trio, rectifier bridge, and stator as covered in *Generator Repair* section.

C. Overcharged Battery

Check battery condition with a suitable battery tester and hydrometer. Excessive water consumption is an indication of overcharging.

1. Connect a voltmeter from generator terminal No. 2 to ground. Meter should indicate battery voltage. A zero reading means that the No. 2 lead is open.
2. If Step 1 is normal but overcharging is evident, proceed as follows:

   a. Disassemble generator as directed and check field windings (rotor) for shorts (Fig. 6-20). If defective, replace both rotor and regulator.
   b. Connect ohmmeter (lowest range) from brush lead clip to end frame as shown in Step 1 of Fig. 6-21. Note reading and then reverse the ohmmeter connections.
   c. If both readings are zero ohms, either the brush lead clip is grounded or the regulator is defective.
   d. A grounded brush lead clip can result from omission of an insulating sleeve. Remove screw to inspect. If satisfactory, replace regulator. See *Generator Repair* Setion.

GENERATOR REPAIR

To repair the generator, observe the following procedure.

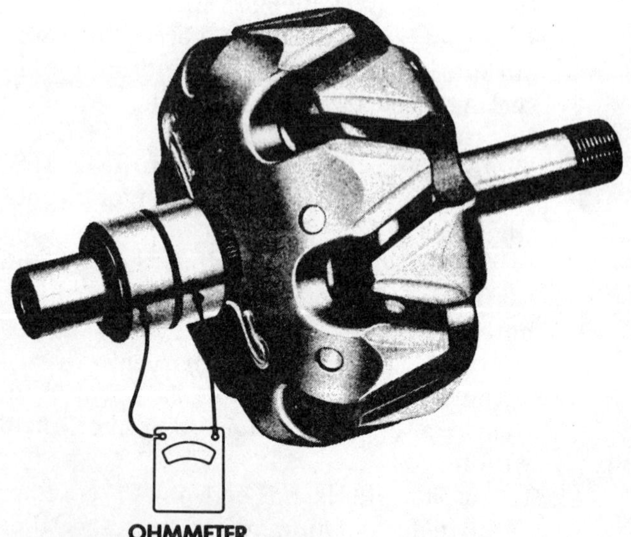

Fig. 6-20. Checking the rotor winding for shorts and opens.

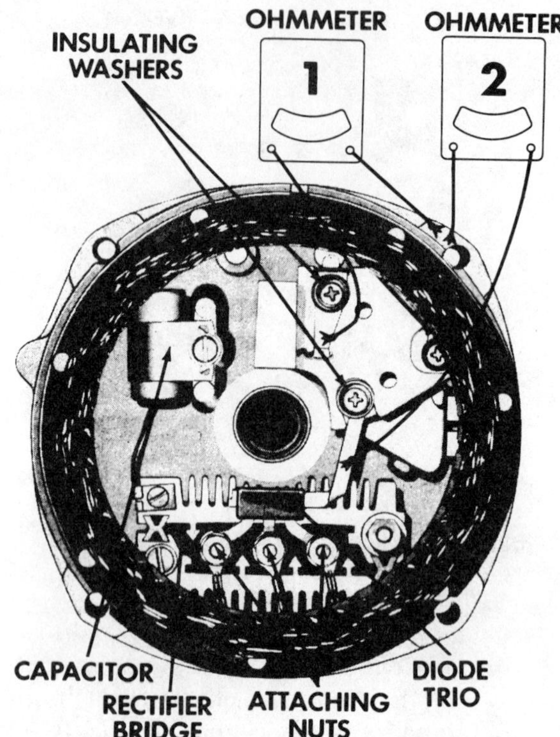

Fig. 6-21. Checking the brush lead clip and regulator with an ohmmeter.

Disassembly

To disassemble the generator, remove the four thru-bolts and separate the drive end frame from the stator assembly by prying apart with a screwdriver at the stator slot. Scribe a line to aid in the alignment of the two halves during reassembly. Tape the slip-ring end-frame bearing and its mating shaft (use pressure-sensitive tape, not friction tape).

To remove the rotor from the end frame, gently clamp the rotor in a vise with just enough pressure to allow removal of the shaft nut. Too much pressure may distort the rotor. When the nut, washer, pulley, fan, and collar are removed, the rotor can be separated from the end frame.

Rotor Field Winding Checks

Check the rotor windings for opens by connecting a test lamp or ohmmeter to the slip rings. If the test lamp fails to light or the ohmmeter indicates infinite resistance, the windings are open. See Fig. 6-20.

Shorts or excessive resistance in the field windings can be detected by connecting the slip rings in series with an ammeter and battery. See Delco-

Remy Service Bulletin 1G-187 for required battery voltage and specified ammeter indications. An ammeter reading above the specified amount indicates a shorted winding; a reading below that specified indicates excessive resistance. An alternate method is to measure rotor resistance with an ohmmeter as described above. However, it will be necessary to convert the specifications in Bulletin 1G-187 to ohms by dividing the listed voltage by the specified current. The result will be the specified resistance of the rotor coil in ohms. If the ohmmeter shows less than the proper resistance reading, the rotor winding is shorted; if the reading is greater, the winding has excessive resistance. Remember, the resistance will vary slightly with temperature.

Diode Trio Check

The diode trio is identified in Fig. 6-21. First, connect an ohmmeter set to its lowest range between the long connector on the diode trio and the generator frame as shown in step 2 of Fig. 6-21. Note the meter reading, then reverse the ohmmeter connections and again note the meter reading. If the readings are the same, check for a grounded brush clip caused by a missing insulator washer (Fig. 6-21) or by a missing or damaged insulator sleeve. If these all check good and the ohmmeter still shows the same readings, replace the regulator.

To check the diode trio, remove it from the end-frame assembly. When doing this, note that the insulating washer on the screw is assembled over the top of the diode trio connector. Connect a low-range ohmmeter as shown in Fig. 6-22. Note the ohmmeter reading, then reverse the leads and again note the reading. Do this for each of the three connectors. One reading should be high and the other reading low for each connector. If any two readings are the same, replace the diode trio. A further check (not shown) is to connect the ohmmeter between each pair of the three connectors. If any reading is zero, replace the diode trio.

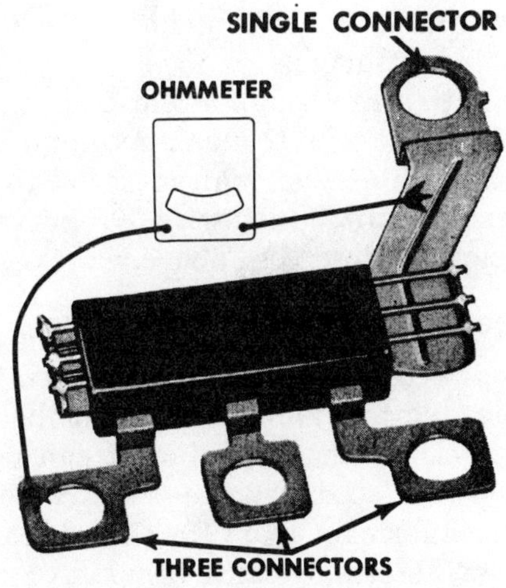

Fig. 6-22. Checking the diode trio.

Rectifier Bridge Check

The rectifier bridge contains a grounded heat sink and an insulated heat sink, the latter being connected to the output BAT terminal. Note that this requires an insulating washer between the insulated heat sink and the end frame.

Check the rectifier bridge by connecting an ohmmeter to the ground heat sink and to any one of the three bridge terminals. See Fig. 6-23. If rectifier is constructed as shown in Fig. 6-24, be sure to press down firmly with the ohmmeter leads on the metal connector and not on the studs. Note the ohmmeter reading, then reverse the test leads and again note the reading. A good rectifier will give one high reading and one low reading at each of the three bridge terminals. Both readings the same at any bridge terminal indicates a defective rectifier. Repeat the above series of checks with the ohmmeter connected to the insulated heat sink and to each of the three bridge terminals. This makes a total of six checks, with two readings for each check.

If a faulty indication is obtained in any one of the above six checks, the rectifier bridge must be

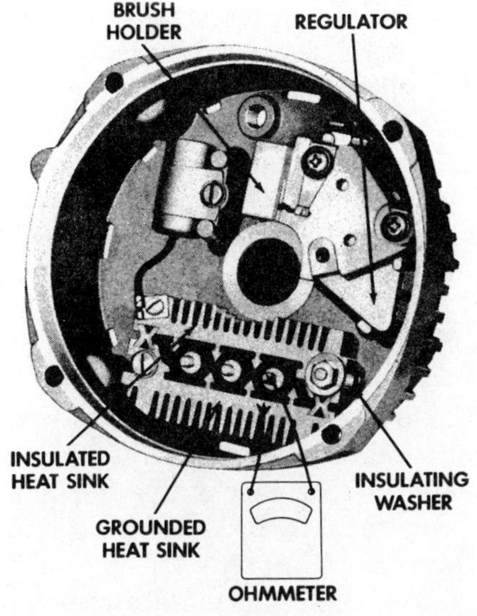

Fig. 6-23. Checking the rectifier bridge.

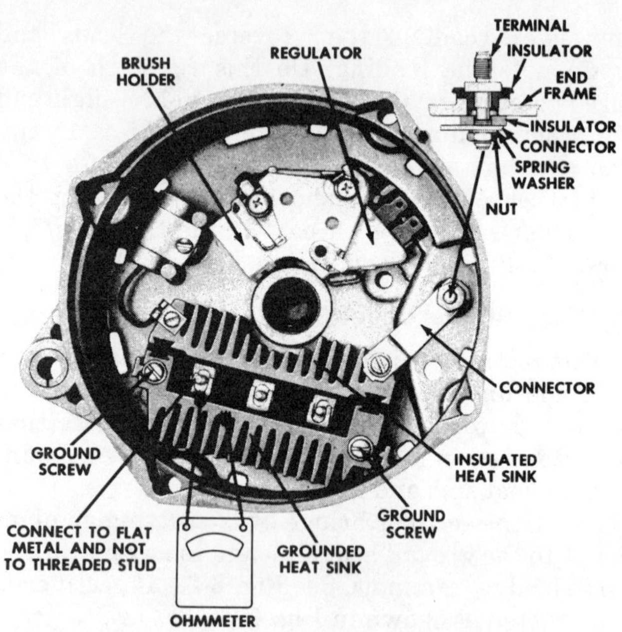

Fig. 6-24. Checking another type of rectifier bridge.

replaced. *CAUTION:* Do not use high voltage, such as a 110-volt test lamp, to test the rectifier bridge.

When replacing the rectifier bridge, note the insulator between the insulated heat sink and end frame. Although rectifiers used in these generators may vary in appearance, they are completely interchangeable.

Stator Checks

The stator windings can be checked with either a test lamp or an ohmmeter. To check for grounds, connect the ohmmeter test leads between stator core and any of the three stator leads. If the lamp lights or the ohmmeter shows low resistance, the windings are grounded. To check for open windings, connect the test leads between any two stator leads (each of three possible combinations must be checked). The lamp should light, or the ohmmeter show low resistance, if there are no opens. (See Fig. 6-25.) NOTE: The delta windings used on 27-SI Series generators cannot be checked for opens.

Due to the low resistance of the stator windings, it is difficult to detect shorted windings. However, if all other electrical checks are normal but the generator still fails to produce the rated output, shorted stator windings (or an open delta winding) are indicated. A shorted stator winding can also cause the indicator lamp to come on at low engine speeds.

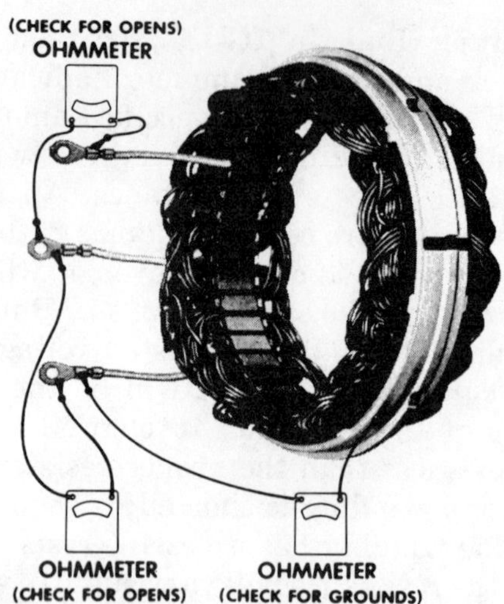

Fig. 6-25. Checking stator windings with an ohmmeter.

Brush Holder and Regulator Replacement

After removing the stator and the diode-trio screw, the brush holder and regulator can be removed by taking out the two retaining screws. Note the two insulators located over the top of the brush clips in Fig. 6-21. The third mounting screw may or may not have an insulator. If not, it must not be interchanged with either one of the other two screws, as a short to ground may result. Regulators used in these generators may vary in appearance, but are completely interchangeable.

Slip-Ring Servicing

Dirty slip rings can be cleaned and finished with 400-grain or finer polishing cloth. Spin the rotor while holding the cloth against the slip rings until they are clean. Attempting to clean the slip rings without spinning the rotor can cause flat spots that result in brush noise.

Slip rings that are rough or out-of-round should be trued in a lathe to .002-inch maximum indicator reading. Remove only enough material to produce a smooth surface and finish with 400-grain or finer polishing cloth as described above.

Bearing Replacement and Lubrication

Remove the drive-end bearing by detaching the retainer plate screws and pressing out the bearing. If it is in satisfactory condition, it can be reused after being lubricated. Fill it one-quarter full with Delco-Remy lubricant No. 1948791 before reassembly. Overfilling may cause bearing to overheat. See Fig. 6-26.

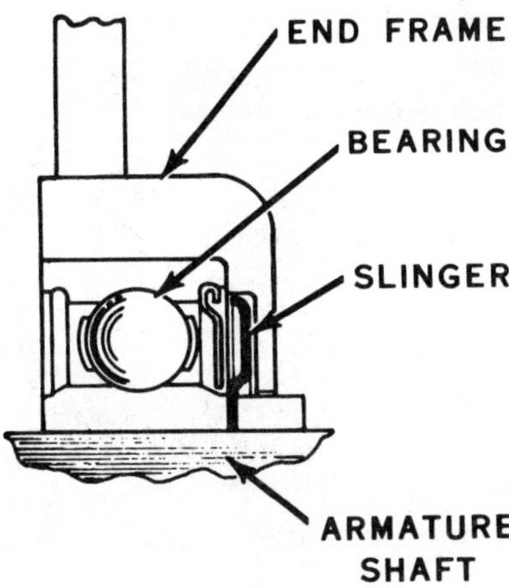

Fig. 6-26. Drive-end bearing assembly.

Install the bearing by pressing it in with a tube or collar that just fits over the outer race. A new retainer plate should be installed if the seal in the original plate is hardened or excessively worn.

The bearing in the slip-ring end frame should be replaced if its grease supply is exhausted. Do not relubricate or reuse this bearing. To remove the bearing, press out with a tube or collar that just fits inside the end-frame housing. Press from the outside. To install a new bearing, place a flat plate over the bearing end and press in from the outside until plate is flush with the end frame. Support the inside of the frame to prevent breakage and misalignment.

It is recommended that a new seal be installed whenever the bearing is replaced. Press in the seal with its lip toward the inside of the end frame. Lightly coat the seal with oil to facilitate reassembly.

Reassembly

Reassemble by reversing the disassembly sequence previously described. When installing the pulley, use only enough vise pressure to permit tightening the shaft nut to 40-60 lb. ft. Excessive pressure may distort the rotor. Remove the protective tape from the bearing and shaft, making sure the shaft is clean. Insert a pin through the hole in the brush holder to hold the brushes in place during reassembly. Carefully install the shaft into the slip-ring end-frame assembly to avoid damage to the seal. After tightening the thru-bolts, remove the brush spring retaining pin to allow brushes to seat on the slip rings.

Generator Bench Check

To check the generator in a test stand, proceed as follows:

1. Make the connections as shown in Fig. 6-27, except leave the carbon pile disconnected. Be sure generator and battery ground polarity are the same. Use a fully charged battery and connect a 10-ohm resistor rated at 6 watts or more between the generator terminal No. 1 and the battery.

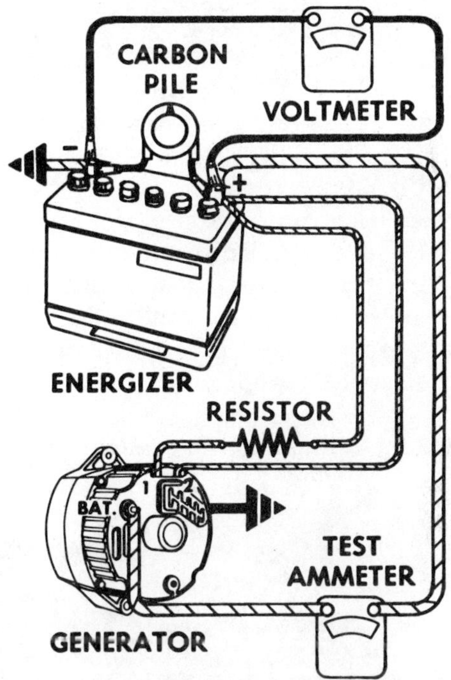

Fig. 6-27. Connections for checking generator output.

2. Slowly increase the generator speed and observe the voltage.
3. If voltage increases above 15.5 volts for a 12-volt system or above 31 volts for a 24-volt system, check for a grounded brush lead clip. If not grounded, replace the regulator and check field winding.
4. If voltage is below the limits in Step 3, connect the carbon pile as shown in Fig. 6-27.
5. With generator operating at moderate speed, adjust carbon pile as needed to obtain maximum output.
6. If output is within 10 percent of the rated output stamped on the generator frame, the generator is good.
7. If output is not within 10 percent of rated

output, keep battery loaded with carbon pile and ground the generator field winding with a screwdriver as indicated in Fig. 6-19.

8. Operate generator at moderate speed and adjust carbon pile for maximum output.
9. If output is now within 10 percent of the rated output, replace the regulator.
10. If output is not within 10 percent of the rated output, check the field winding, diode trio, rectifier bridge, and stator winding as previously described.

DELCOTRON GENERATORS 10-DN SERIES, 100, 112, 130, 133 TYPES

An external view of a typical Delcotron generator is shown in Fig. 6-28, a cross-sectional view is illustrated in Fig. 6-29, and a wiring diagram is shown in Fig. 6-30.

Since the Delcotron generator and regulator are designed for use with only one system polarity, the following precautions *must* be observed when working on the charging circuit. Failure to observe these precautions will result in serious damage to the electrical equipment.

1. When installing a battery, always make absolutely sure the ground polarity of the battery and the ground polarity of the Delcotron generator are the same.
2. When connecting a booster battery, make certain to connect the negative battery terminals together and the positive battery terminals together.
3. When connecting a charger to the battery, connect the positive charger lead to the positive battery terminal and the negative charger lead to the negative battery terminal.
4. Never operate the Delcotron generator on open circuit. Make absolutely certain all connections in the circuit are clean and tight.
5. Do not short across or ground any of the terminals on the Delcotron generator or regulator.
6. Do not attempt to polarize the Delcotron generator.

TESTS AND MAINTENANCE

Even though the Delcotron generator is constructed to give long periods of trouble-free service, a regulator inspection procedure should be followed to obtain the maximum life from the generator.

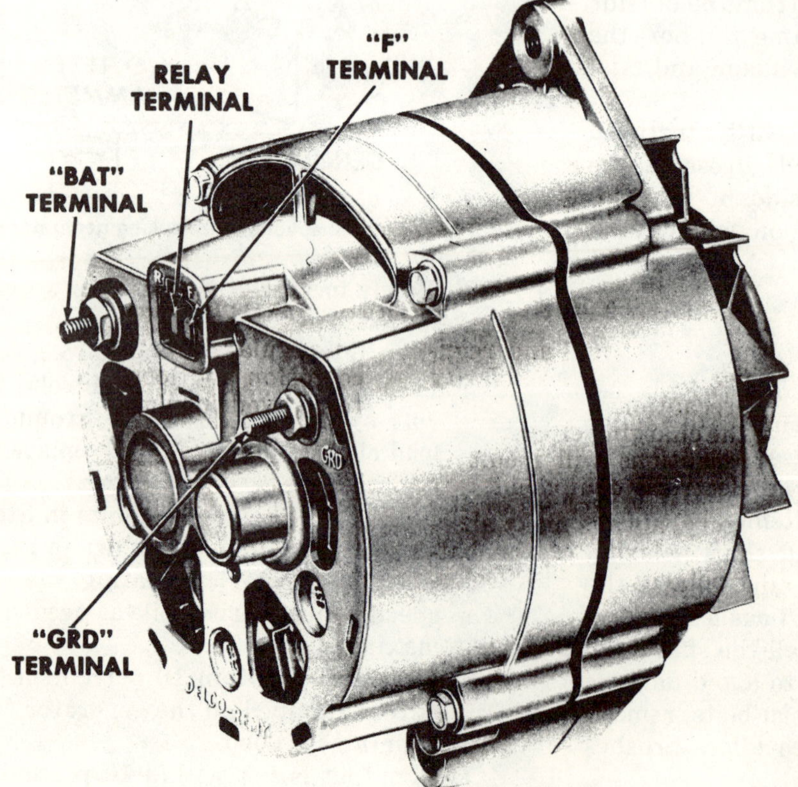

Fig. 6-28. Delcotron 10-DN Series generator.

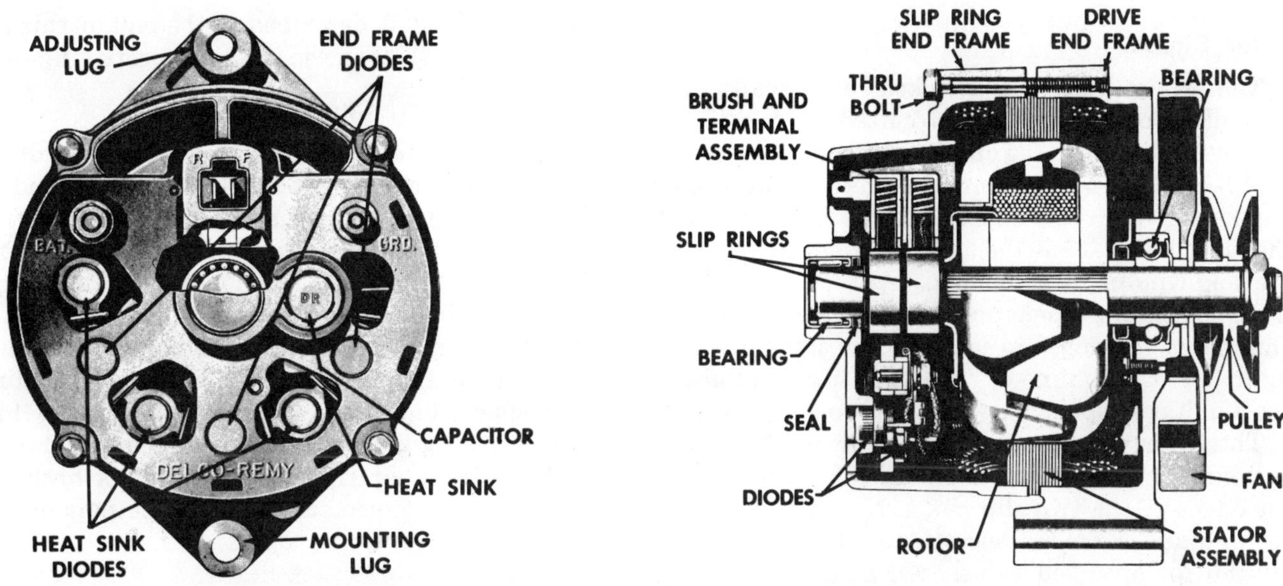

Fig. 6-29. End view and cross-sectional view of 10-DN Series Delcotron generator.

Inspection

The frequency of inspection is determined largely by the type of operating conditions. High-speed operation, high temperatures, and dust and dirt all increase the wear of brushes, slip rings, and bearings.

At regular intervals, inspect the terminals for corrosion and loose connections, and inspect the wiring for frayed insulation. Check the mounting bolts for tightness, and the belt for alignment, proper tension, and wear. Belt tension should be adjusted in accordance with manufacturer's recommendations. When tightening belt tension, apply pressure against the stator laminations between the end frames, and not against either end frame.

Noisy Generator

Noise from a Delcotron generator may be caused by worn or dirty bearings, loose drive pulley, a defective diode, or a defective stator.

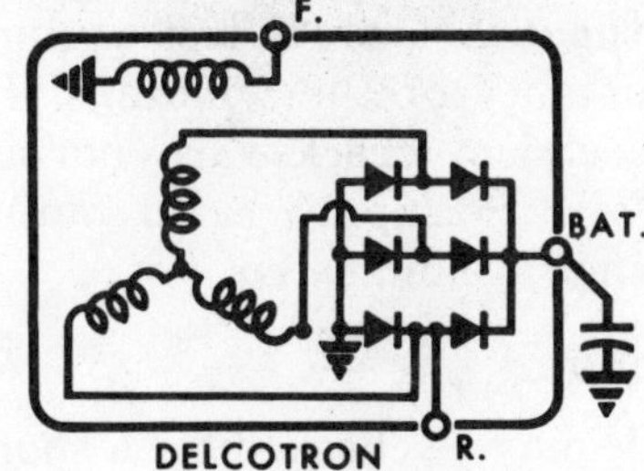

Fig. 6-30. Wiring diagram for Delcotron 10-DN Series generator.

Disassembly

After extended periods of operation, or at time of engine overhaul, the Delcotron generator may be removed from the vehicle for a thorough inspection and cleaning of all parts. The Delcotron consists of four main components—the two end frames, the stator, and the rotor.

To disassemble the Delcotron generator take out the four thru-bolts, and separate the drive end frame and rotor assembly from the stator assembly by prying apart with a screwdriver at the stator slot. A scribe mark will help locate the parts in the same position during reassembly. The fit between stator and frame is not tight, and the two can be separated easily. Note that the separation is to be made between the *stator frame* and *drive end frame*. After disassembly, place a piece of tape over the slip-ring end-frame bearing to prevent entry of dirt and other foreign material, and also place a piece of tape over the shaft on the slip-ring end. If brushes are to be reused, clean with a soft dry cloth. *CAUTION:* Use pressure-sensitive tape and not friction tape which would leave a gummy deposit on the shaft.

To remove the drive end frame from the rotor, place the rotor in a vise and tighten only enough to permit removal of the shaft nut. *CAUTION:* Avoid excessive tightening as this may cause distortion of the rotor. Remove the shaft nut, washer, pulley, fan, and the collar, and then separate the drive end frame from the rotor shaft.

Rotor Checks

The rotor may be checked electrically for grounded, open, or short-circuited field coils as shown in Fig. 6-31. To check for grounds, connect a 110-volt test lamp or an ohmmeter from either slip ring to the rotor shaft or to the rotor poles. If the lamp lights, or if the ohmmeter reading is low, the field winding is grounded.

To check for opens, connect the test lamp or ohmmeter to each slip ring. If the lamp fails to light, or if the ohmmeter reading is high (infinite), the winding is open.

The rotor winding is checked for short circuits by connecting a battery and ammeter in series with the edges of the two slip rings. Note the ammeter reading and refer to Delco-Remy Service Bulletin 1G-186 for specified values. An ammeter reading above the specified value indicates shorted windings. An alternate method is to check the resistance of the field by connecting an ohmmeter to the two slip rings. If the resistance reading is below the specified value, the winding is shorted. The specified resistance value can be determined by dividing the specified voltage by the current given in Bulletin 1G-186.

If the rotor winding is not defective, and the Delcotron generator fails to supply rated output when checked as described at the end of this chapter, the trouble is in the stator or rectifying diodes.

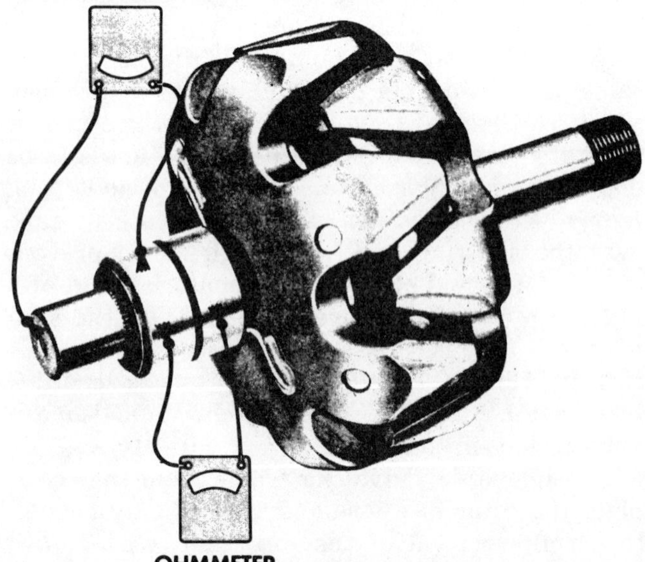

Fig. 6-31. Checking the rotor winding for opens, grounds, and shorts.

Stator Winding Checks

To check the stator windings, remove all three stator-lead attaching nuts (Fig. 6-32), and then separate the stator assembly from the end frame. The fit between the stator frame and the end frame is not tight, and the two can be separated easily.

The stator windings may be checked with a 110-volt test lamp or an ohmmeter as shown in Fig. 6-33. If the lamp lights, or if the meter reading is low when connected from any stator lead to the frame, the windings are grounded. If the lamp fails to light, or if meter reading is high when successively connected between each pair of stator leads, the windings are open.

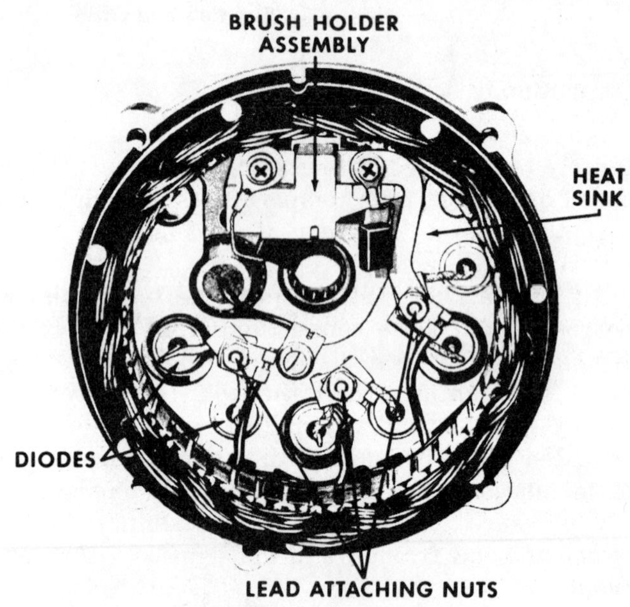

Fig. 6-32. View of stator assembly with slip-ring end frame removed.

A short circuit in the stator windings is difficult to locate without laboratory test equipment due to the low resistance of the windings. However, if all other electrical checks are normal and the generator fails to supply rated output, shorted stator windings are indicated.

Diode Checks

Each diode may be checked for a shorted to open condition using any one of the methods outlined below.

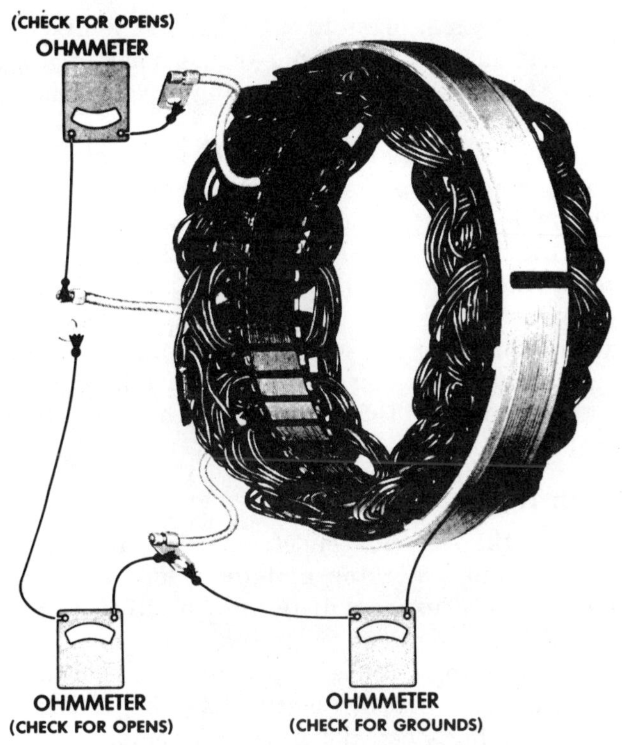

Fig. 6-33. Checking the stator winding.

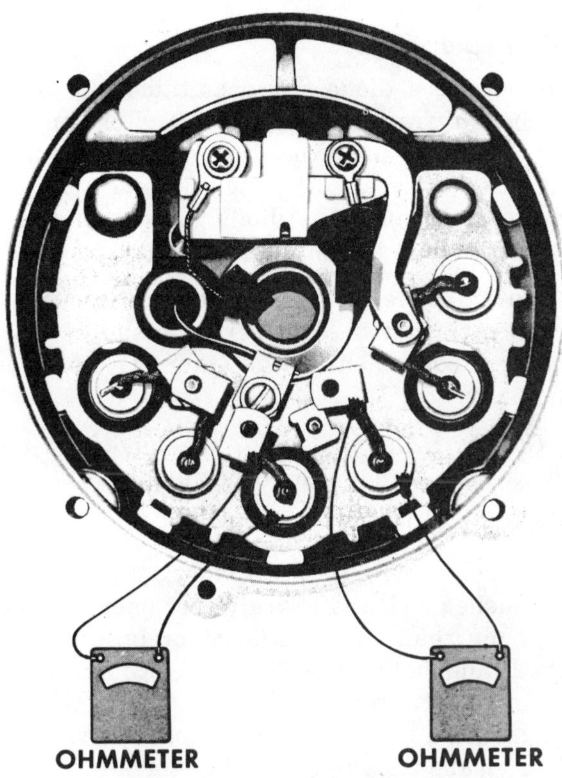

Fig. 6-34. Checking the diodes.

Ohmmeter Method

One method of checking the diodes is to use an ordinary ohmmeter. The lowest range on the ohmmeter should be used, and the ohmmeter should have a 1.5-volt cell. To determine the cell voltage, turn the selector to the lowest scale, and then connect the ohmmeter leads to a voltmeter. The voltmeter will indicate the cell voltage for most ohmmeters.

With the stator windings disconnected, check the diodes in the heat sink by connecting one of the ohmmeter leads to the heat sink, and the other ohmmeter lead to one of the diode leads as shown in Fig. 6-34, and note the reading. Then reverse the ohmmeter lead connections and note the reading. If both readings are very low, or if both reading are very high, the diode is defective. A good diode will give one low reading and one high reading. Check the other two diodes in the heat sink in the same manner.

To check the diodes mounted in the end frame, connect one of the ohmmeter leads to the end frame, and the other ohmmeter lead to one of the diode leads (Fig. 6-34), and note the reading. Then reverse the ohmmeter lead connections and note the reading. Again, if both readings are very low, or if both readings are very high, the diode is defective. A good diode will give one low reading and one high reading. Check the other two diodes mounted in the end frame in the same manner.

Test-Lamp Method

An alternate method of checking the diodes is to use a test lamp of not more than 12 volts in place of the ohmmeter.

Caution: Do not use a 110-volt test lamp to check the diodes.

With the stator windings disconnected, connect the test lamp leads across each diode as previously described, first in one direction and then in the other direction. If the lamp lights in both directions, or fails to light in either direction, the diode is defective. When checking a good diode, the lamp will light in only one of the two directions.

Special Tester Method

Special testers are available which check the diodes without disconnecting the stator windings. To use these testers, follow the tester manufacturer's recommendations.

Diode Replacement

To remove a diode, use a suitable tool to support the end frame or heat sink, and use an arbor press or vise to push the diode out. To replace a diode, use a special tool which fits over the outer diode edge to push the diode in, supporting the heat sink or end frame with a suitable tool.

NOTE: Diode replacement tools are available from various manufacturers that supply tools and test equipment to the automotive service industry.

Caution: Do not strike the diode, as the shock may damage the other diodes.

Slip-Ring Servicing

If the slip rings are dirty, they may be cleaned and finished with 400-grain or finer polishing cloth. Spin the rotor in a lathe, or by some other method, and hold the polishing cloth against the slip rings until they are clean. *CAUTION:* The rotor must be rotated in order that the slip rings will be cleaned evenly. Cleaning the slip rings by hand without spinning the rotor may result in flat spots on the slip rings, causing brush noise.

Slip rings which are rough or out-of-round should be trued in a lathe to .002-inch maximum indicator reading. Remove only enough material to make the rings smooth and round. Finish with 400-grain or finer polishing cloth and blow away all dust.

Bearing Replacement and Lubrication

The bearing in the drive end frame can be removed by detaching the retainer plate screws, and then pressing the bearing from the end frame. If the bearing is in satisfactory condition, it may be reused by filling it one-quarter full with Delco-Remy lubricant No. 1948791 before reassembly. *CAUTION:* Do not overfill, as this may cause the bearing to overheat. Sealed bearings must be replaced.

To install a new bearing, press in with a tube or collar that just fits over the outer race. It is recommended that a new retainer plate be installed if the felt seal in the original retainer plate is hardened or excessively worn.

The bearing in the slip-ring end frame should be replaced if its grease supply is exhausted. No attempt should be made to relubricate and reuse the bearing. To remove the bearing from the slip-ring end frame, press it out with a tube or collar that just fits inside the end-frame housing. Press from the outside of the housing toward the inside.

To install a new bearing, place a flat plate over the bearing and press in from the outside toward the inside of the frame until the bearing is flush with the outside of the end frame. Support the inside of the frame with a hollow cylinder to prevent breakage of the end frame. Use extreme care to avoid misalignment or otherwise placing undue stress on the bearing. Saturate the felt seal with S.A.E. 20 oil, and then reassemble the felt seal and steel retainer.

Brush Replacement

When the slip-ring end-frame assembly is separated from the rotor and drive end-frame assembly, the brushes will fall down onto the shaft and come in contact with the lubricant. If the brushes are to be reused, they must be thoroughly cleaned with a soft dry cloth. Also, the shaft must be thoroughly cleaned before reassembly.

The brush springs should be inspected for any evidence of damage or corrosion. If there is any doubt as to the condition of the brush springs, they should be replaced.

To install new brushes, remove the two screws that attach the brush-holder assembly to the end frame. Install the springs and brushes into the brush holder, and insert a straight wire or pin into the holes at the bottoms of the brush holders to retain the brushes. Then attach the brush-holder assembly onto the end frame, noting carefully the proper order of parts as shown in Fig. 6-35. Allow the straight wire to protrude through the hole in the end frame.

Heat Sink Replacement

In order to replace the heat sink, remove the BAT and GRD terminals from the end frame, and the

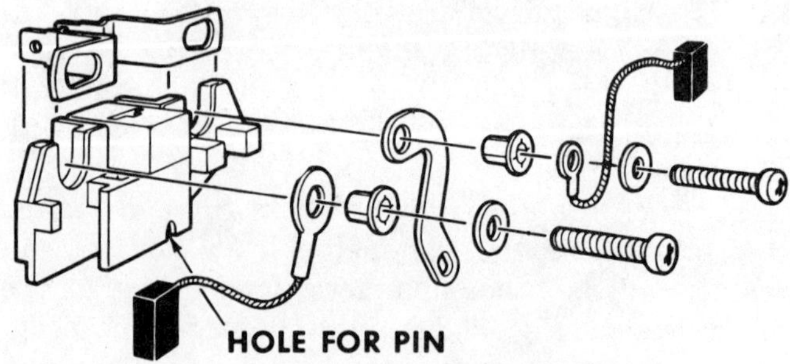

Fig. 6-35. Exploded view of the brush-holder assembly.

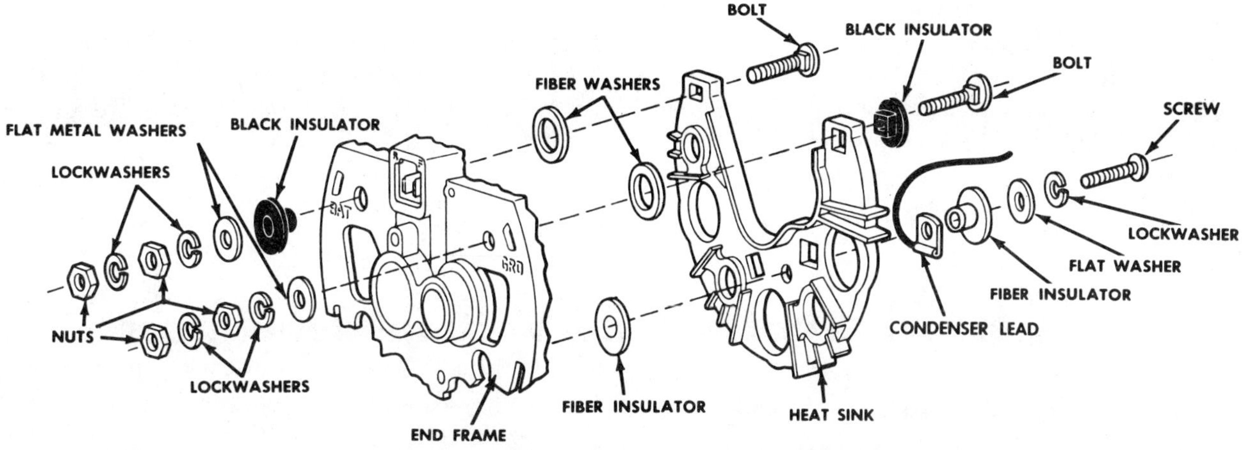

Fig. 6-36. Exploded view of the heat-sink assembly.

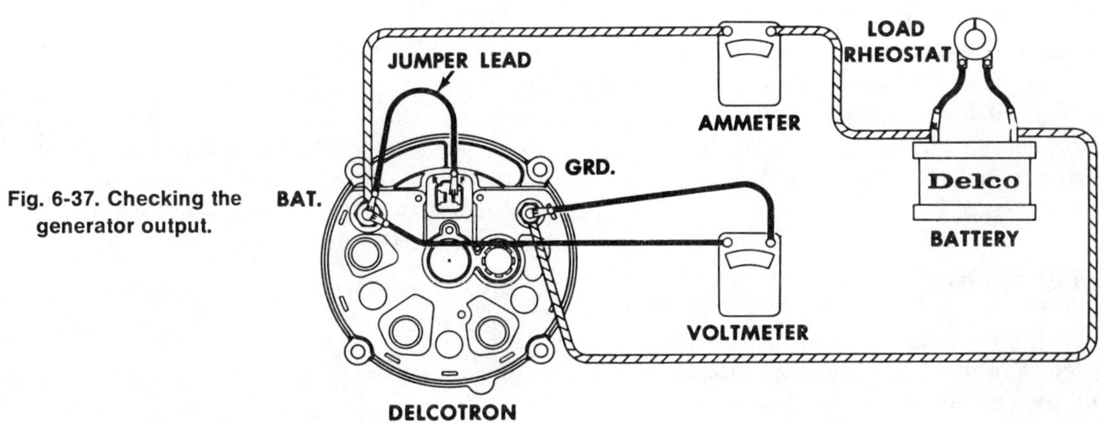

Fig. 6-37. Checking the generator output.

screw attaching the condenser lead to the heat sink. During reassembly, note carefully the proper order of parts as shown in Fig. 6-36.

Reassembly

Reassembly is the reverse of disassembly. Remember when assembling the pulley to secure the rotor in a vise with just enough pressure to permit tightening the shaft nut to 50-60 ft. lbs. If excessive pressure is applied against the rotor, the assembly may become distorted.

To install the slip-ring end-frame assembly to the rotor and drive end-frame assembly, remove the protective tape over the bearing and shaft. Make sure that the shaft is perfectly clean after removing the tape.

Insert a straight wire as described previously through the holes in the brush holder and end frame to retain the brushes in the holder. Then withdraw the wire after the Delcotron generator has been completely assembled. The brushes will then drop onto the slip rings.

Output Check

To check the output of the Delcotron generator on a test bench, make electrical connections as shown in Fig. 6-37. Operate the generator at the specified speed and check for the rated output as given in Delco-Remy Service Bulletin 1G-186. Adjust the load rheostat, if necessary, to obtain the desired output. Note: A special adapter which can be used for making connections to the Delcotron generator is available from tool companies and test equipment manufacturers normally supplying equipment to the automotive service trade.

> *CAUTION:* On negative-ground Delcotron generators, connect the negative battery post to the generator frame, and on positive-ground units, connect the positive battery post to the frame.

CHAPTER 7

Chrysler Alternators and Voltage Regulators

GENERAL INFORMATION

The alternator contains six built-in silicon rectifiers to convert the ac current generated in the stator windings to the dc current that flows from the output terminal. The main components of the alternator are the rotor, stator, rectifiers, end shields, and the drive pulley. These components are shown in Figs. 7-1 and 7-2.

REGULATOR OPERATION

The electronic voltage regulator regulates the electrical-system voltage by limiting the output voltage generated by the alternator. This is accomplished by controlling the amount of current that is allowed to flow through the alternator field winding. The electronic voltage regulator has no moving parts and requires no adjustment after it is set at the factory. The components in the regulator include transistors, diodes, some resistors, and a capacitor.

Basically, the electronic regulator operates as a voltage-sensitive switch. There is a power transistor in series with the alternator field winding and a control circuit that senses the system voltage. This control circuit turns the power transistor on and off as required to maintain the desired voltage level. As alternator speed and electrical-system load conditions change, the control circuit turns the power transistor on and off many times a second. The only time the transistor is not turning on and off is during low engine speeds and high electrical loads. Under these conditions, the transistor is on continuously to supply steady field current to the alternator.

One important feature of the electronic regulator is its ability to vary the regulated system voltage up or down as the temperature changes. This provides the optimum charging conditions for the battery throughout the seasons of the year.

SERVICE PROCEDURES

Circuit Resistance Test

The charging-circuit resistance test will show the amount of voltage drop (or loss) between the alternator output terminal and the battery. Use the following procedure for this test:

1. Disconnect the battery ground cable.
2. Disconnect the BAT lead at the alternator output terminal.
3. Connect a test ammeter with an adequate range in series with the charging circuit at the alternator output terminal. See Fig. 7-3.
4. Connect the leads of a test voltmeter as shown in Fig. 7-3; connect the positive lead to the alternator output terminal and the negative lead to positive battery post.
5. Disconnect the green regulator field wire from the alternator.

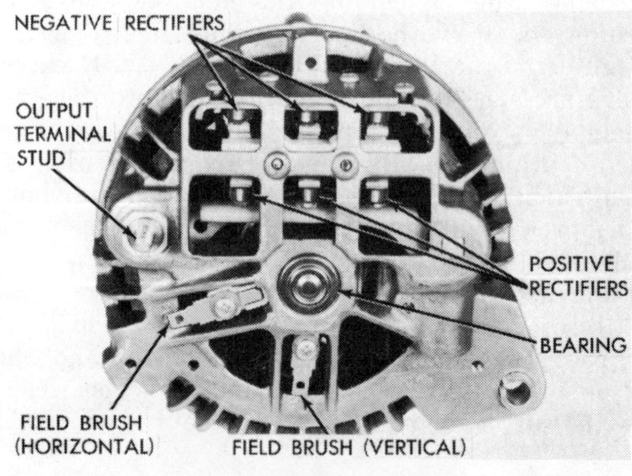

Fig. 7-2. Alternator components viewed from end frame.

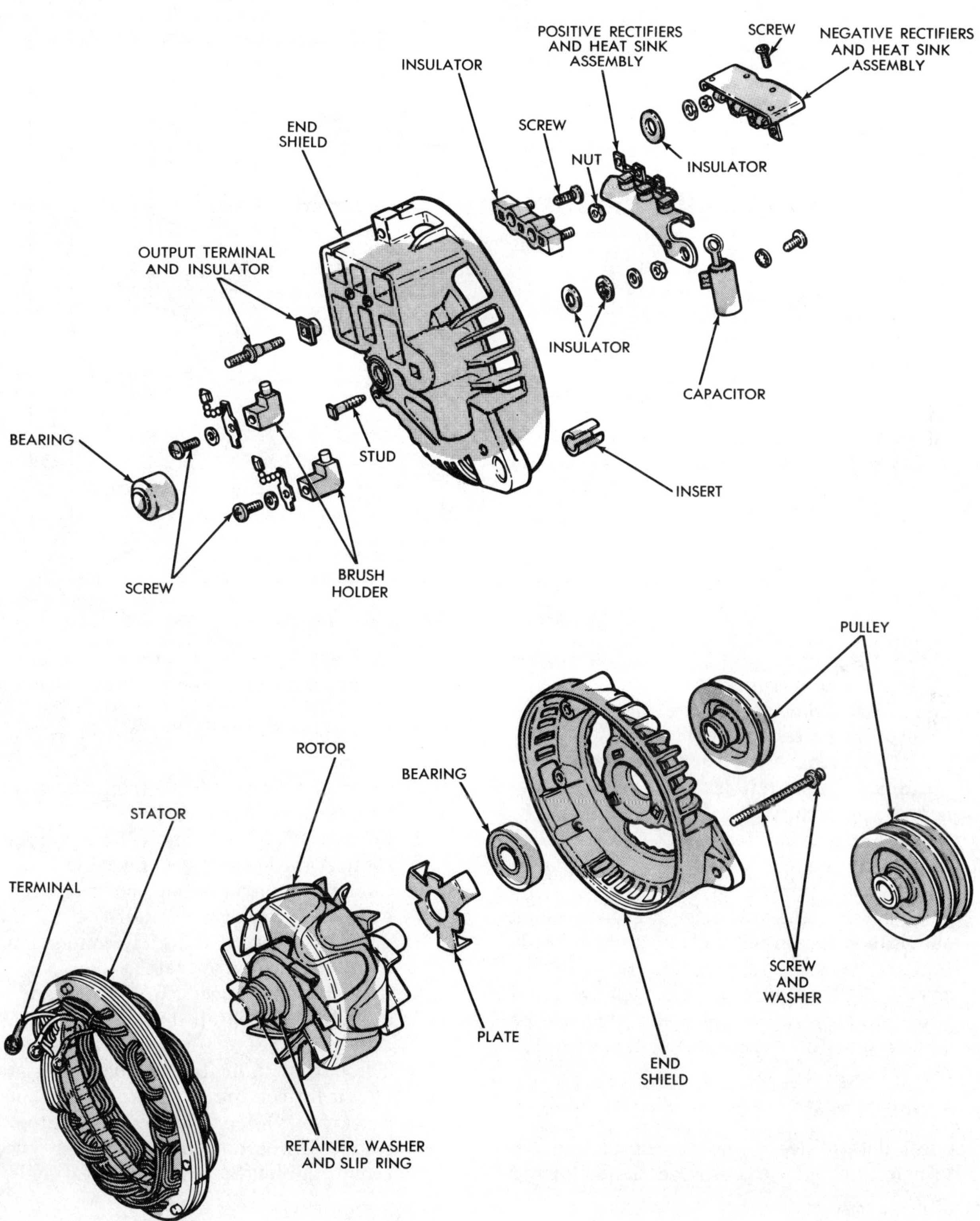

Fig. 7-1. Exploded view of the alternator.

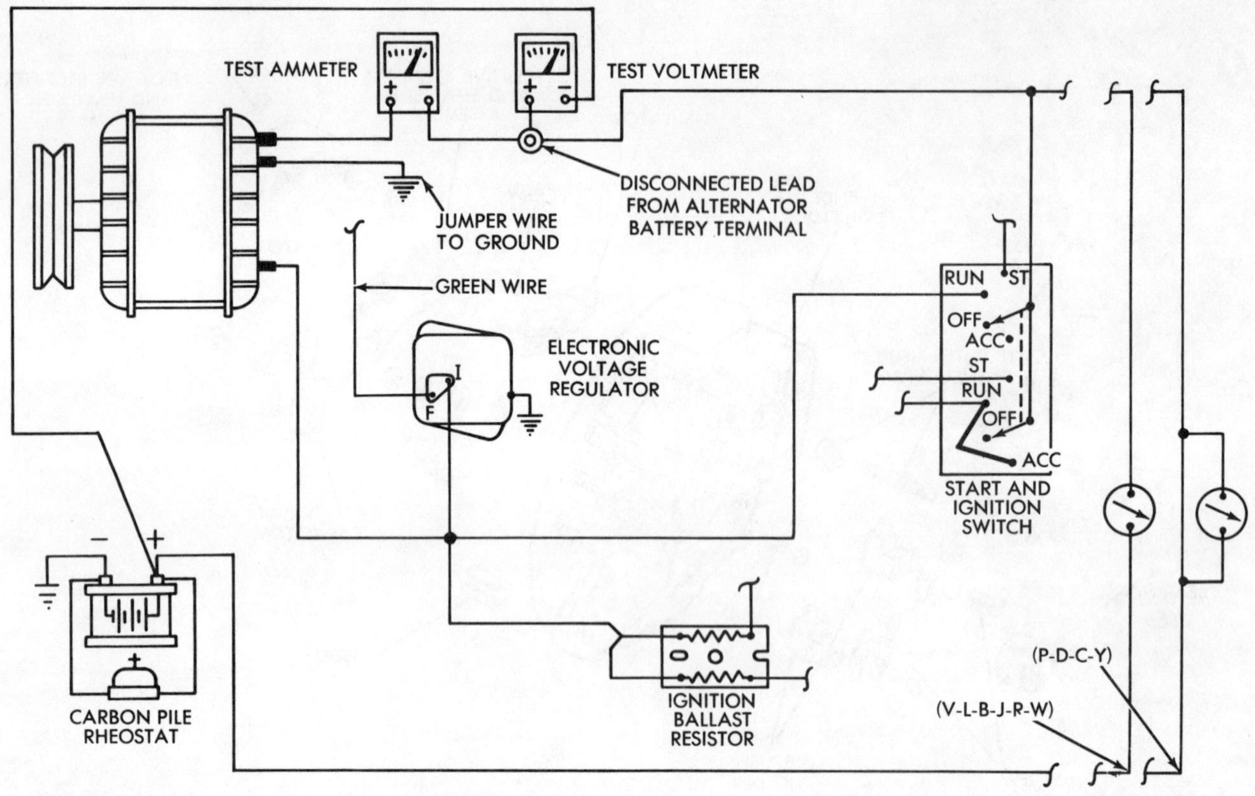

Fig. 7-3. Test connections for circuit resistance test.

6. Connect a jumper lead from the alternator field terminal to ground.
7. Connect a tachometer to the engine and reconnect the battery ground lead.
8. Connect a variable carbon pile to the battery terminals. Be sure it is in the OFF position before connecting.
9. Operate engine at idle speed.
10. Adjust engine speed and the carbon pile to maintain 20 amperes of current in the circuit. Observe the voltmeter reading, which should not exceed 0.7 volt. If the voltage is higher, check for poor connections in the circuit between alternator output terminal and the battery. The voltmeter can also be used to pinpoint excessive resistance in each portion of the circuit.

Current Output Test

This test determines if the alternator can deliver its rated output current. Use the following procedure for the current output test.

1. Disconnect battery ground cable.
2. Connect an ammeter into circuit as in the previous test.
3. Connect a test voltmeter to the alternator output terminal and ground as shown in Fig. 7-4.
4. Disconnect the green field wire at the alternator.
5. Connect a jumper lead from the alternator field terminal to ground.
6. Connect a tachometer to the engine and reconnect the battery ground cable.
7. Connect a variable carbon pile across the battery terminals. Be sure it in the OFF position before making the connection.
8. Start engine and operate at idle.
9. Adjust engine speed to 1250 rpm and adjust carbon pile to obtain 15 volts as indicated on the voltmeter.
10. The output indicated by the ammeter must be within the limits shown in the specifications for the particular alternator being tested. If the output is less than specified, remove alternator for bench testing.

Voltage Regulator Test

1. The specific gravity of the battery must be above 1.200 for a proper voltage regulator test.

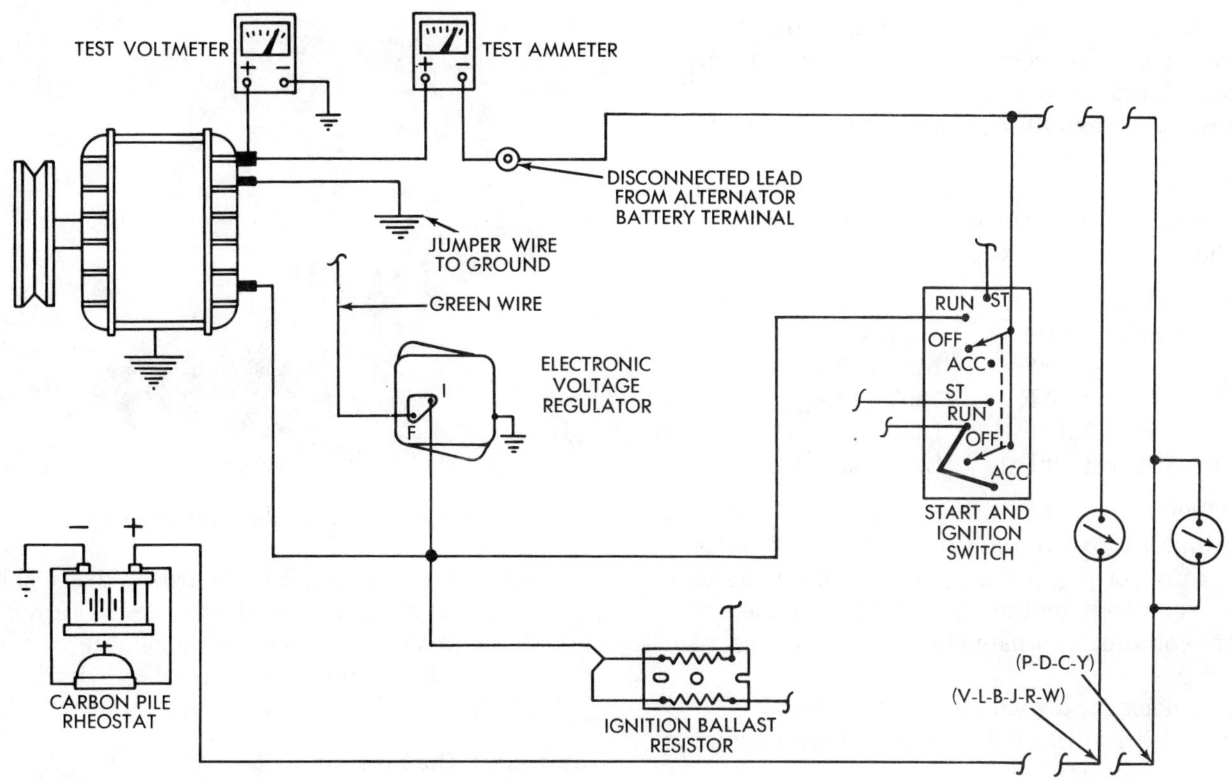

Fig. 7-4. Test connections for alternator current output test.

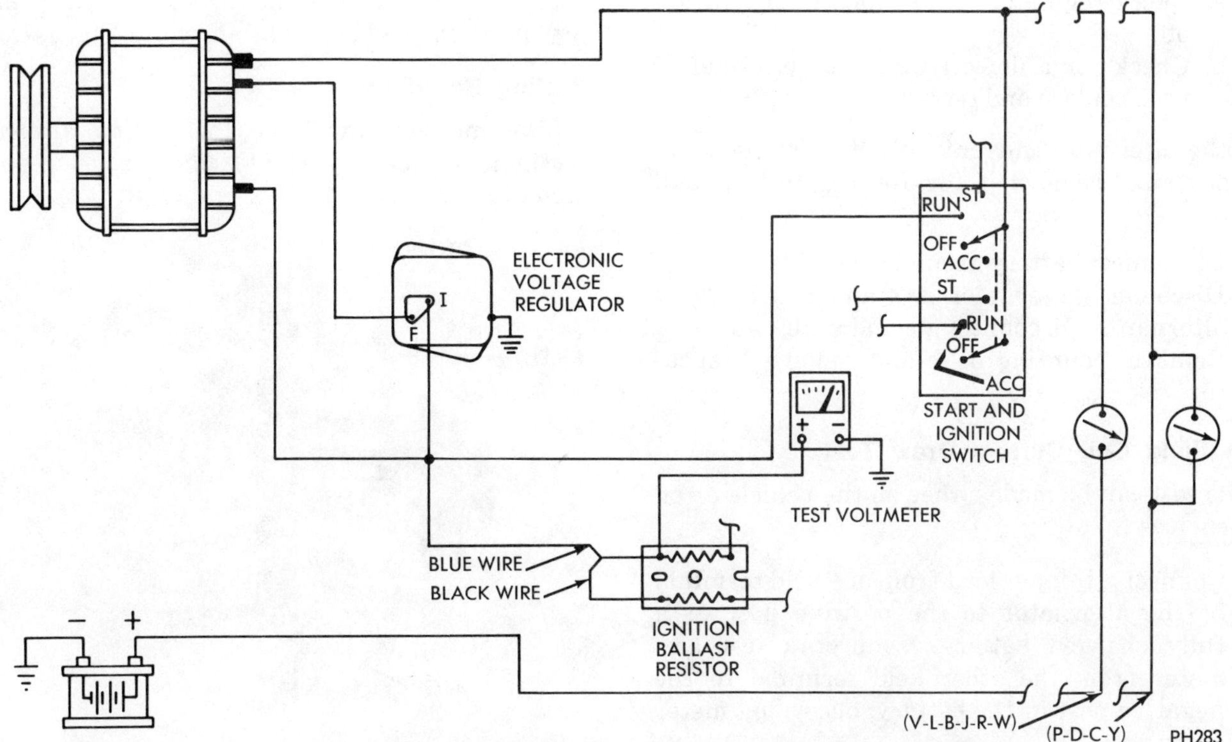

Fig. 7-5. Test connections for voltage-regulator check.

2. Connect the test voltmeter to the ignition terminal on the regulator (or other specified test point) and to ground. See Fig. 7-5. Be sure the regulator is properly connected to the alternator.
3. Operate engine at 1250 rpm with all lights and accessories turned off. Indicated voltage should be within range shown:

Ambient Temp. near regulator	*Voltage Range*
−20°F	14.3—15.3
80°F	13.8—14.4
140°F	13.3—14.0
Above 140°F	Less than 13.8

   Allow sufficient running time (typically 2—5 minutes) for voltage to stabilize. If battery is considerably discharged, a longer time may be required for the voltage to stabilize.
4. If voltage is unsteady or below specified range:
   a. Check for a good regulator ground.
   b. With ignition off, check voltage regulator connections.
   c. Check for a defective regulator. If defective, replace and retest.
5. If the voltage is above the specified limits:
   a. Check regulator connections with ignition off.
   b. Check for a defective regulator. If defective, replace and retest.

If the alternator current output does not meet specifications, remove it for further testing and service.

1. Disconnect battery ground cable.
2. Disconnect alternator BAT and FLD leads at alternator. Disconnect ground wire.
3. Remove mounting bolts and remove alternator.

Rotor Field Coil Current Draw Test

This test can be made either on the vehicle or on the bench as follows:

1. Connect a jumper lead from one field terminal of the alternator to the positive post of a fully charged battery. Connect a test ammeter from the other field terminal to the negative post of the battery, observing meter polarity.
2. Slowly rotate the rotor by hand and observe

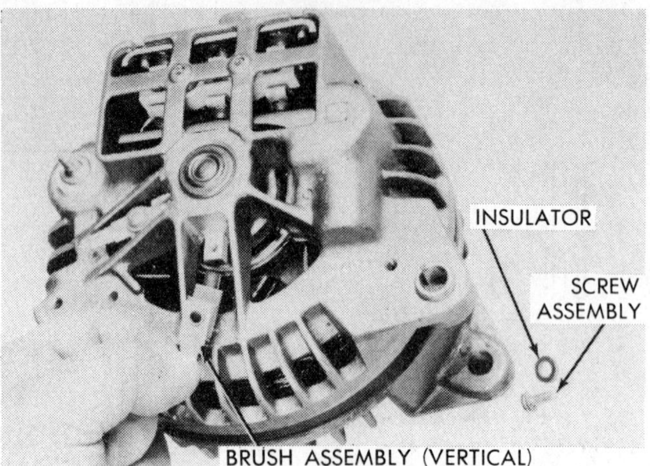

Fig. 7-6. Removing the brush assembly.

ammeter reading. Field current draw should be 2.5 to 3.7 amperes at 12 volts. A high draw indicates a possible shorted winding whereas a low draw indicates excessive winding resistance. Zero current means an open field.

Alternator Disassembly

To prevent possible damage to brush assemblies, remove them before disassembling the alternator. Proper removal of the brush assembly is shown in Fig. 7-6. Next, remove the thru-bolts and carefully pry apart the end shield as shown in Fig. 7-7.

Testing Rectifiers

Two methods available for testing alternator rectifiers (diodes) are: (1) commercial in-circuit diode testers and (2) test lamp and battery. The

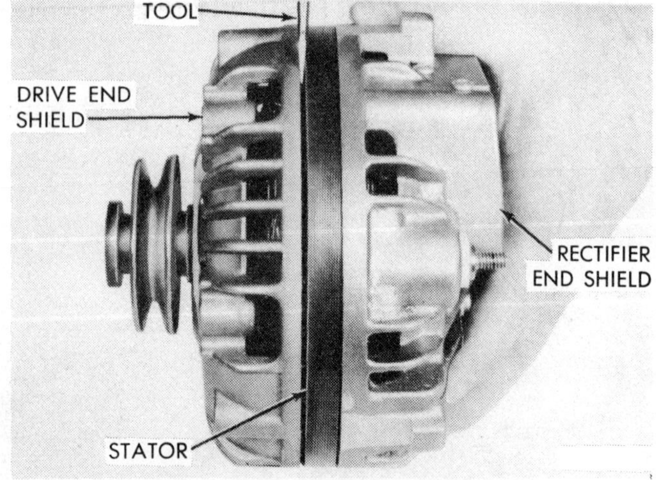

Fig. 7-7. Separating the end shield from the alternator assembly.

advantage of the first method is that the rectifiers can be checked without disconnecting the stator winding leads from the rectifier assembly. The second method requires that the stator winding be disconnected.

1. Disconnect and remove the stator from the end shield as shown in Fig. 7-10.
2. Connect a test lamp (No. 67 or similar lamp) in series with a 12-volt battery and two test leads.

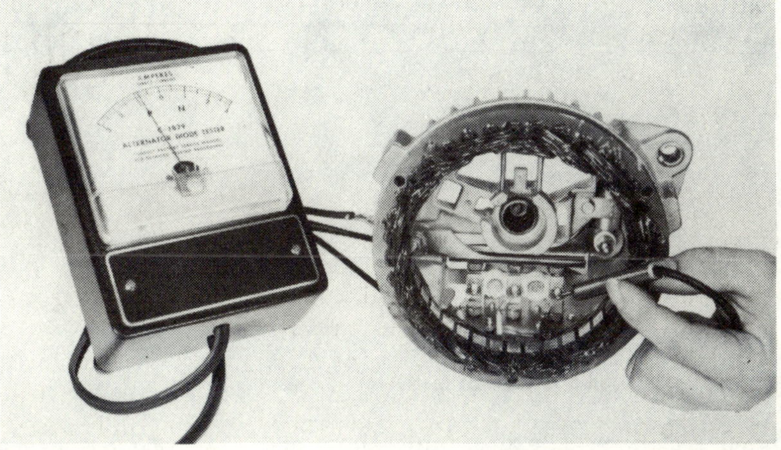

Fig. 7-8. Checking the diodes in the positive cluster.

Full instructions for using in-circuit diode testers are usually provided with the instrument. In general, the procedure involves connecting one test lead to the output terminal and touching the other test lead to each of the three stator leads. The meter reading indicates if the diodes are good or bad. The same procedure is used to test the grounded diodes by connecting one of the test leads to the alternator frame and again touching the other test lead to each stator connection. Figs. 7-8 and 7-9 show such an in-circuit diode tester in use.

If such a tester is not available, the test-lamp method can be used with the following procedure.

3. Connect one test prod to the alternator output terminal and touch the other prod to each of the three stator connection terminals on the rectifier assembly as shown in Fig. 7-11. Reverse the test-prod connections and repeat the above procedure. The normal indication with good rectifiers is for the lamp to light with one test-prod polarity but for it to remain off with the other polarity. A defective rectifier will cause the lamp to either remain off or remain on with the test prods in both polarities.
4. Repeat Step 3, but connect one of the test prods to the alternator frame. This tests the

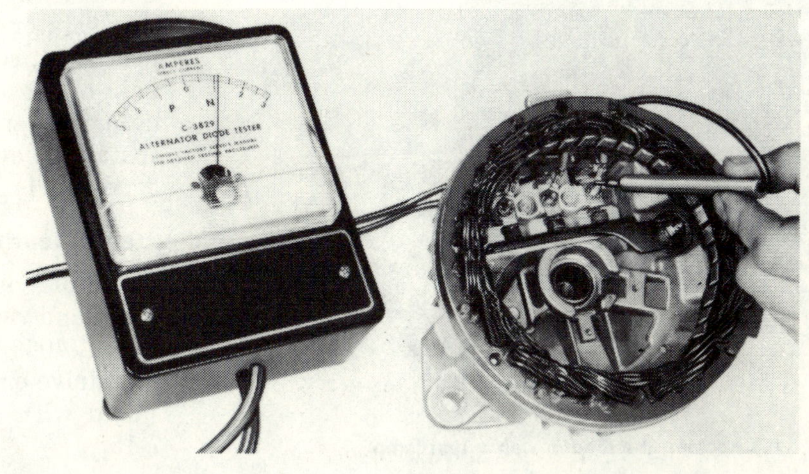

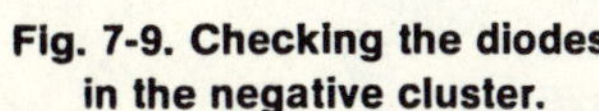

Fig. 7-9. Checking the diodes in the negative cluster.

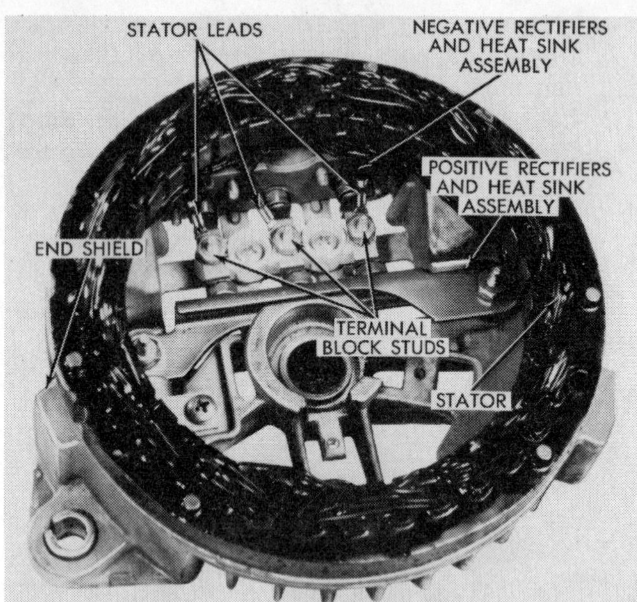

Fig. 7-10. Location of the stator leads.

grounded rectifiers. The test indications are the same as for Step 3.

Rectifier and Heat Sink Removal

1. Loosen the four hex-head screws holding the negative rectifier and heat sink assembly to the rectifier end shield. Completely remove the outer two screws and lift the assembly out of the end shield. See Fig. 7-12.
2. Remove the two nuts and washers holding the positive rectifier and heat sink assembly to the insulated terminals in the rectifier end shield. Remove the capacitor mounting screw. Lift out insulated washer, capacitor, and positive rectifier and heat sink assembly.

Fig. 7-11. Checking the diodes with a test lamp.

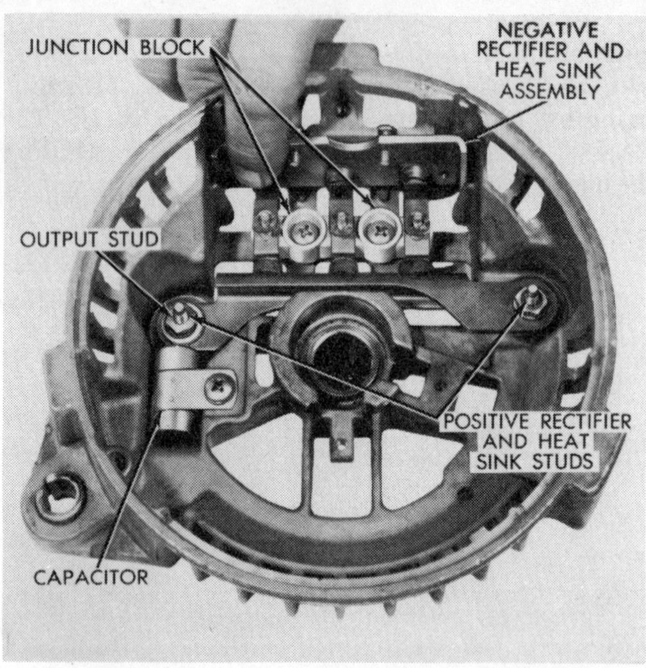

Fig. 7-12. Removing the rectifier and heat sink assembly.

Testing the Stator Windings

The stator can be tested using the same test-lamp arrangement that was used for testing the rectifiers.

1. Press one test prod firmly onto pin of the stator frame as shown in Fig. 7-13.
2. Press the other test prod firmly onto each of the three stator leads, one at a time. If the lamp lights, the stator is grounded.
3. Contact the test prods to any two of the three stator leads. The lamp should light. Repeat this procedure for each of the other two pair of stator leads. Failure of the lamp to light indicates an open stator winding.
4. Install a new stator if an open or grounded condition is indicated.

Pulley and Bearing Removal

1. The pulley is an interference fit on the rotor shaft and requires a special puller (Chrysler Tool C-4068, see Fig. 7-14).
2. Pry drive-end bearing retainer from the end shield with a screwdriver as shown in Fig. 7-15.

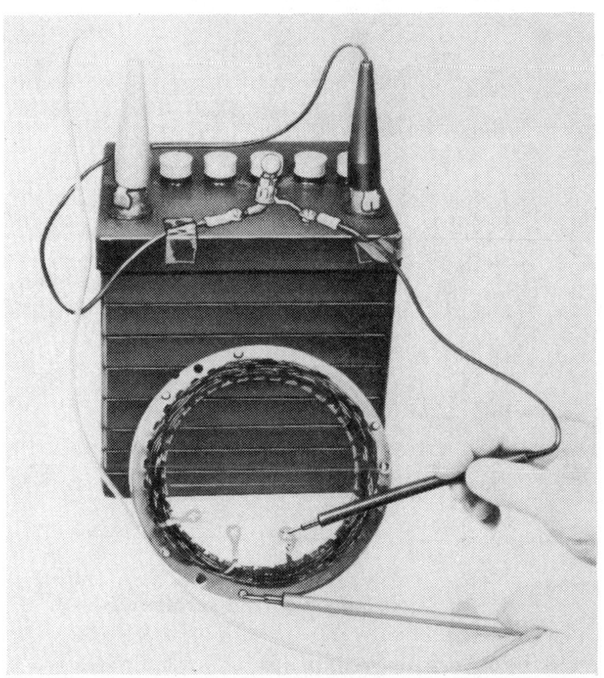

Fig. 7-13. Checking for grounded stator windings.

3. Support end shield and tap rotor shaft with a plastic hammer to separate rotor from end shield.
4. Remove the drive-end ball bearing with C-4068 tool as shown in Fig. 7-16.

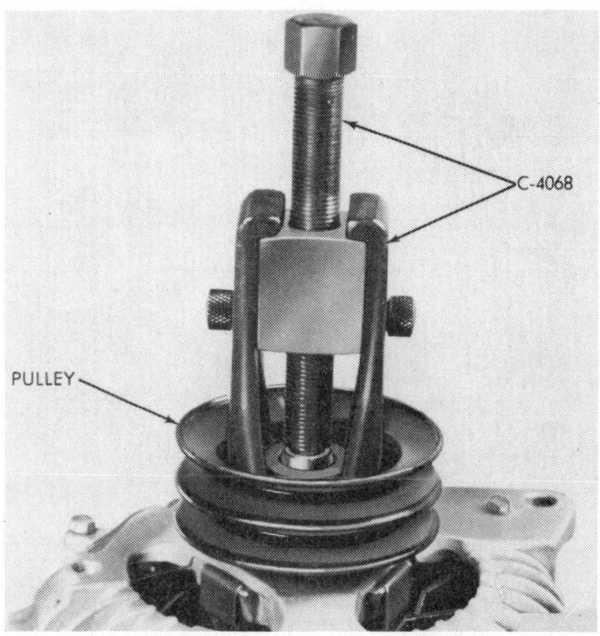

Fig. 7-14. Removing the alternator pulley.

5. The needle roller bearing is a press fit. When necessary to remove, use tools shown in Fig. 7-17.

Rotor Test

The rotor assembly can be checked for grounded, open, or shorted field coils by use of an ohmmeter.

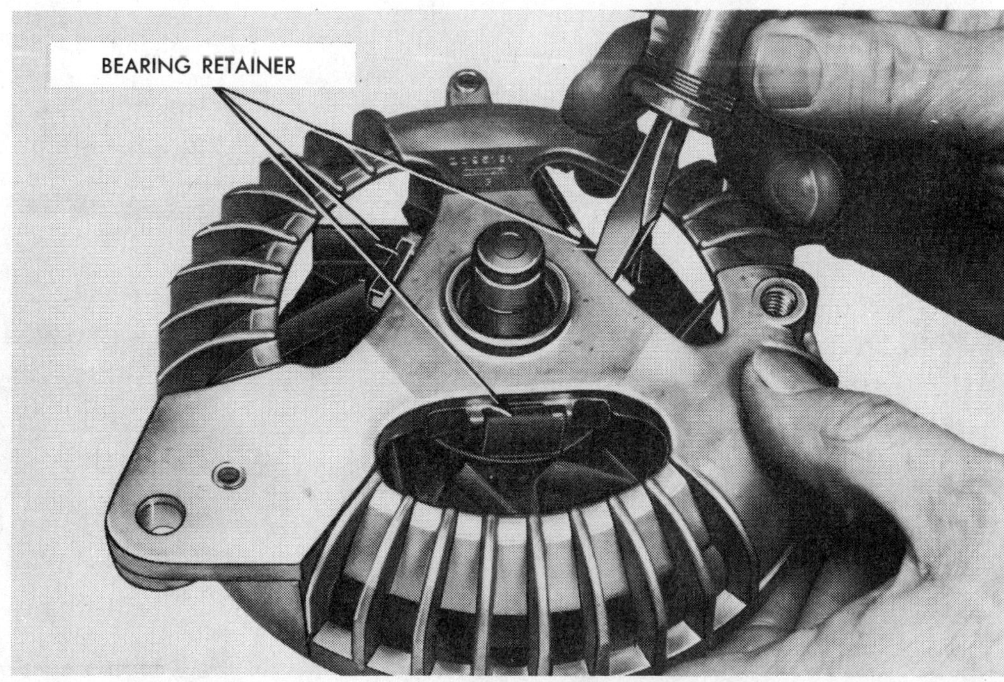

Fig. 7-15. Removing the bearing retainer.

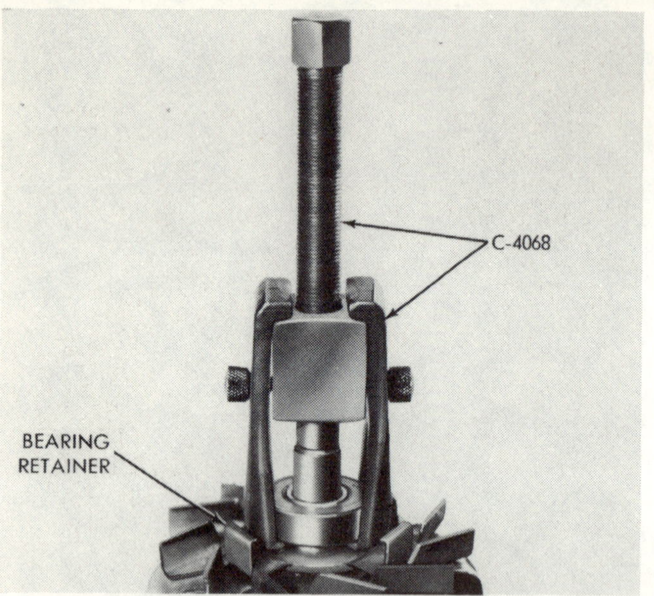

Fig. 7-16. Removing drive-end ball bearing.

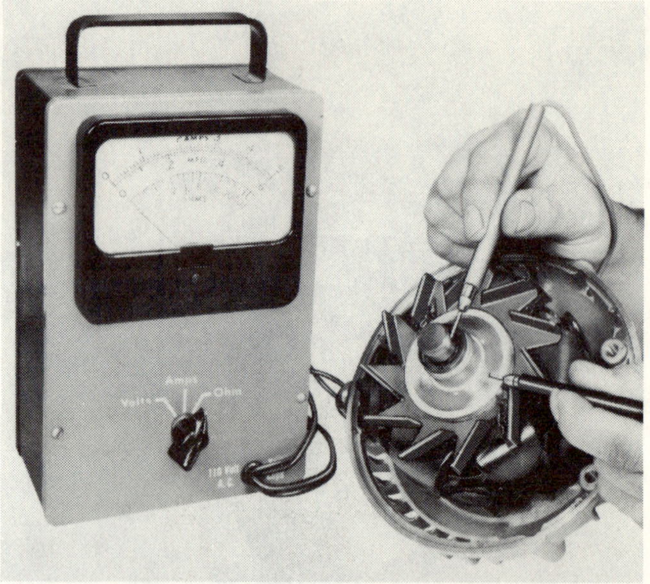
Fig. 7-18. Checking for grounded rotor winding.

To check for a grounded rotor winding, connect the ohmmeter prods to one of the slip rings and to the rotor shaft as shown in Fig. 7-18. If no grounds are present, the meter will show infinite resistance. Any reading other than infinite indicates a grounded, or partially grounded, rotor winding.

To check for an open rotor winding, connect the ohmmeter prods to both slip rings as shown in Fig. 7-19. The meter should indicate about 3 to 4 ohms (or specified value) if there are no opens. A reading of infinite resistance indicates an open winding. A higher-than-normal reading indicates excessive winding resistance. A lower-than-normal reading could be caused by a shorted winding. Remember, the resistance varies with temperature, increasing as the temperature increases.

Replacing Slip Rings

To replace damaged slip rings, proceed as follows:

1. Remove plastic grease retainer from rotor.
2. Unwind field-coil leads from slip-ring lugs, being careful not to break the leads.

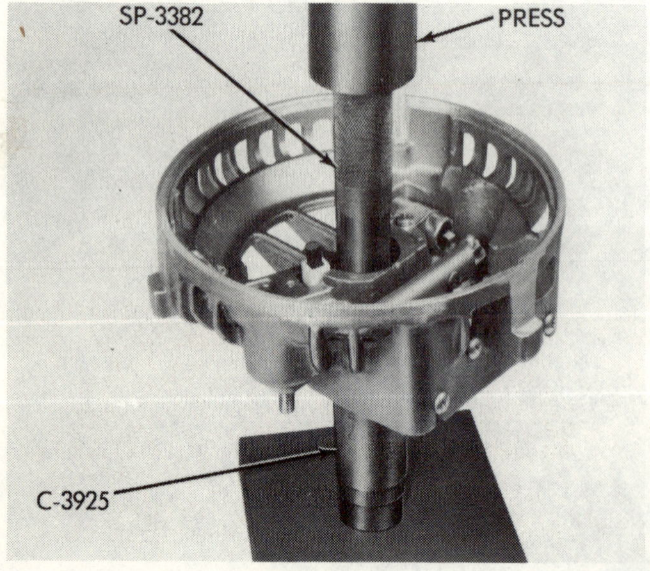

Fig. 7-17. Removing the needle bearing.

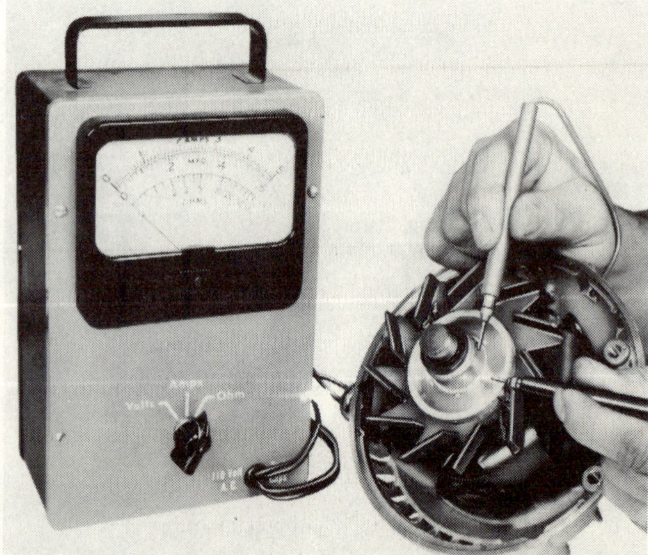
Fig. 7-19. Measuring resistance of rotor winding.

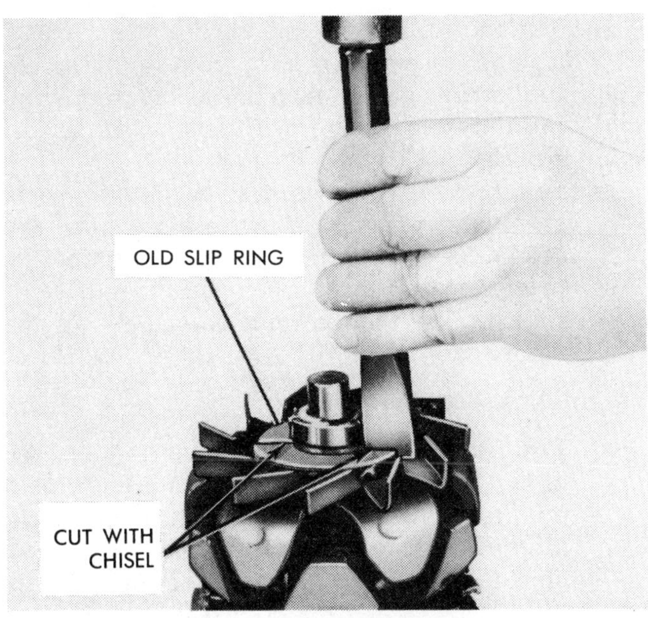

Fig. 7-20. Removing the slip rings.

3. Use a chisel to cut through the copper of both slip rings at opposite points (180 degrees apart) as shown in Fig. 7-20.
4. Break the plastic insulator and remove the old slip ring.
5. Clean away dirt and particles of old slip rings from rotor.
6. Scrape ends of field coil leads for good electrical contact.
7. Position field-coil leads to provide a clear path for the new slip ring.

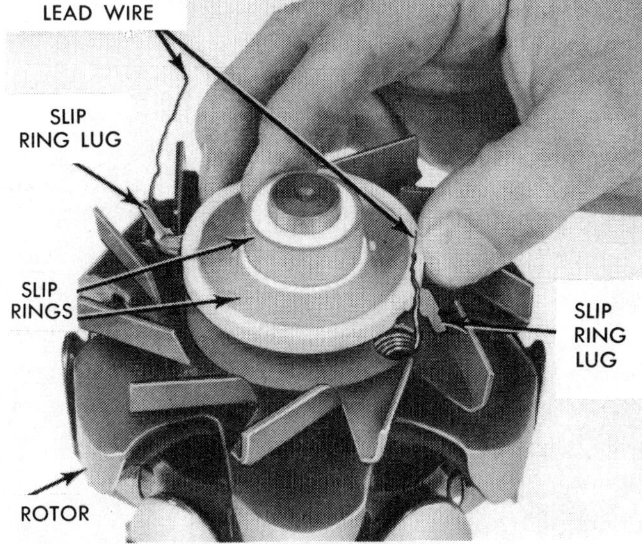

Fig. 7-21. Positioning the new slip rings.

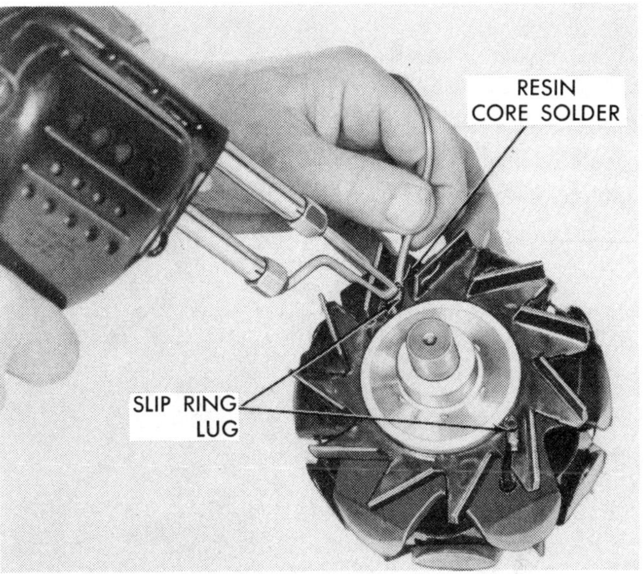

Fig. 7-22. Pressing slip rings onto shaft.

8. Position new slip ring carefully on the shaft to ensure that slip-ring lugs will be in proper position for connecting field leads. See Fig. 7-21.
9. Place special tool (C-3900) over rotor shaft and position rotor, slip ring, and tool assembly in an arbor press as shown in Fig. 7-22. Press slip ring onto shaft. Be sure that the field lead for the insulated-brush ring clears the access hole, the fan, and the pole piece.

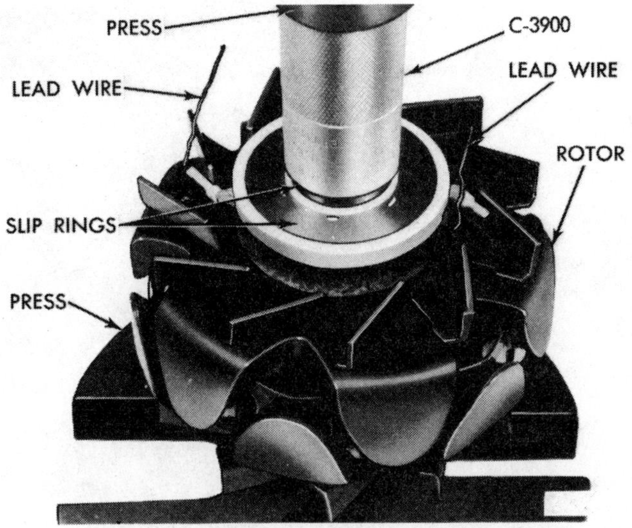

Fig. 7-23. Soldering rotor windings to slip-ring lugs.

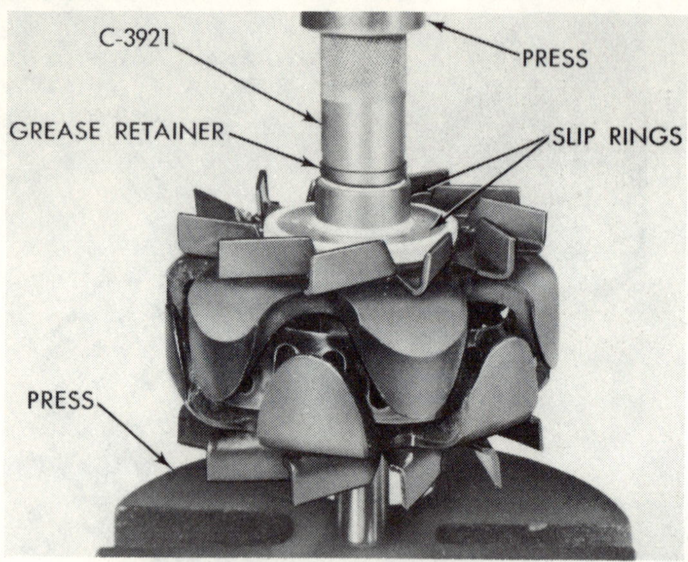

Fig. 7-24. Installing grease retainer.

10. Tin each field lead and then coil each lead around its respective slip-ring lug, starting first wrap against shoulder of lug and winding outward. Solder with rosin-core solder. See Fig. 7-23.
11. Position the grease retainer on the rotor shaft and press on with installer tool (C-3921) as shown in Fig. 7-24. Retainer is properly positioned when the inner bore of the installer tool bottoms on the end of the rotor shaft.

Assembling the Alternator

1. Position rectifier-end-shield bearing on base of tool (C-4201). Place alternator end shield on top of bearing so that it is properly aligned. With top part of tool placed on end shield, press bearing into place until it bot-

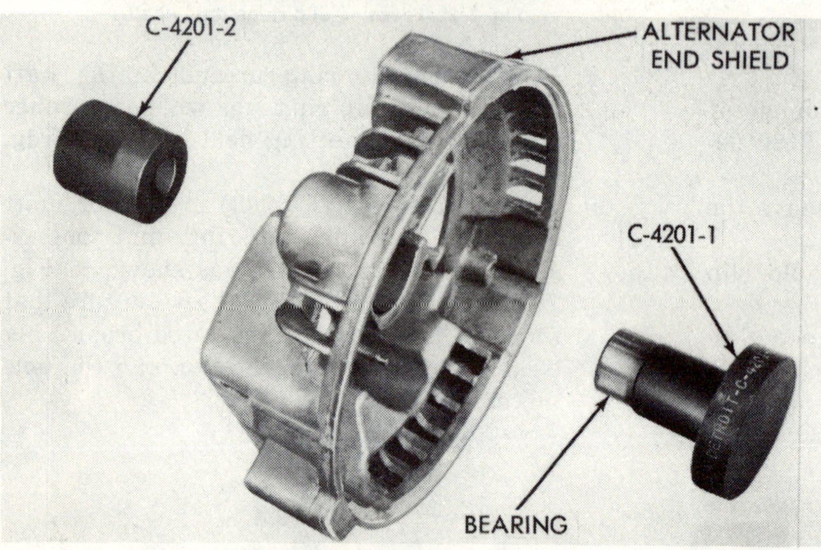

Fig. 7-25. Installing rectifier-end-shield bearing.

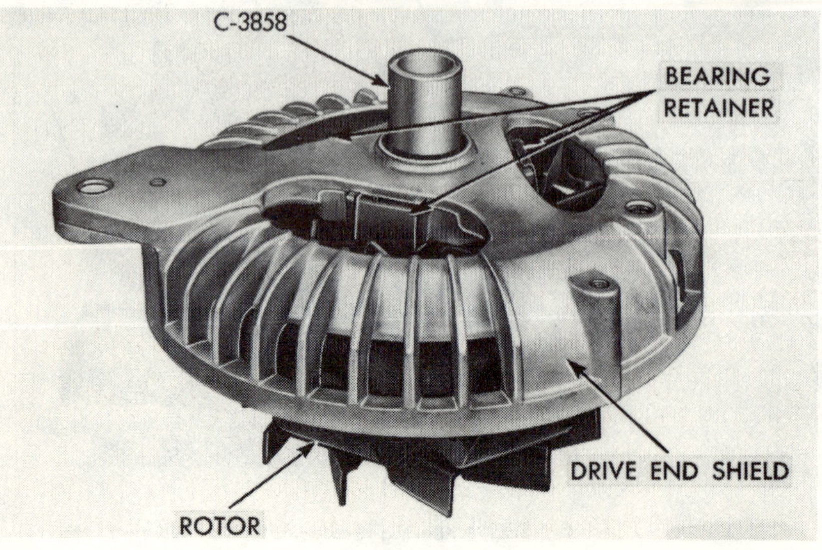

Fig. 7-26. Pressing drive-end bearing onto rotor shaft.

Fig. 7-27. Installing pulley on rotor shaft.

toms against the end shield. See Fig. 7-25. New bearings are prelubricated.

2. Insert drive-end-shield bearing in drive-end bearing shield and install bearing retainer plate to hold bearing in place.
3. Position bearing and drive-end shield on rotor shaft and, while supporting base of rotor shaft, press bearing-end shield into position on rotor shaft with arbor press and special tool (C-3858). Press bearing onto shaft until it contacts shoulder on rotor fan hub. See Fig. 7-26.

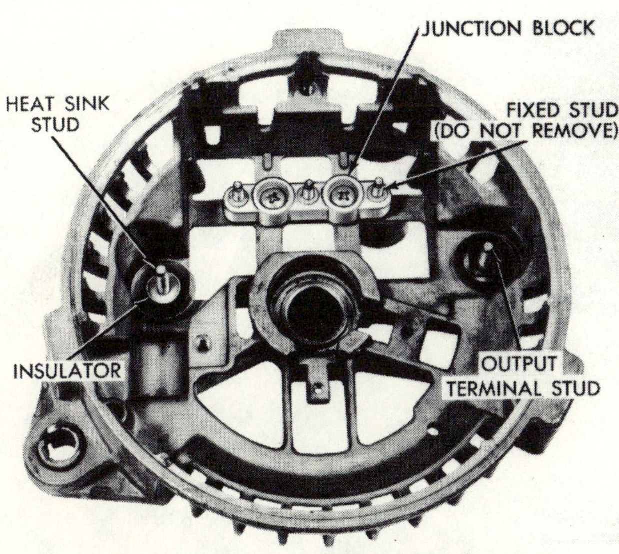

Fig. 7-28. Installing output terminal stud.

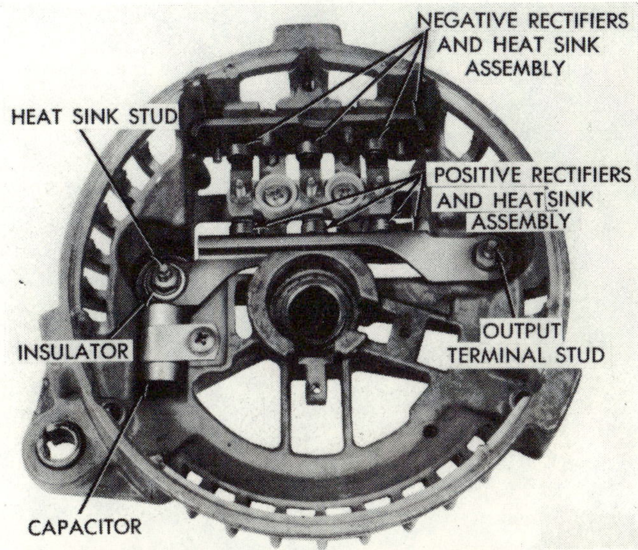

Fig. 7-29. Installing rectifier and heat sink assembly.

4. Install pulley on rotor shaft. Shaft of rotor must be supported in a manner so that all pressing force is on the pulley hub and rotor shaft. See Fig. 7-27. Press pulley on shaft until it contacts the inner race of the drive end bearing.
5. If removed, install output terminal stud and insulator through the end shield. Be sure mica insulators are in place and undamaged (Fig. 7-28). Install positive heat sink assembly over studs; guide rectifier straps over studs on terminal block.
6. Install capacitor terminal over capacitor end stud. Install capacitor shoulder insulator. Ground capacitor bracket to end shield with capacitor mounting screw. Install and tighten positive heat sink nut and lockwasher assemblies.
7. Slide negative rectifier and heat sink assembly into place in end shield. Position rectifier straps on terminal junction block studs. Install hex-head metal screws through end shield and into negative heat sink and tighten securely. See Fig. 7-29.
8. Position stator over rectifier-end shield and install winding terminals on terminal block. Press stator alignment pins into end shield and install and tighten winding terminal nuts. Route leads so that they cannot contact rotor or sharp edge of negative heat sink.
9. Position rotor and drive-end shield assembly over stator and rectifier-end shield assembly. Align thru-bolt holes in both end shields.
10. Compress both end shields manually and install thru-bolts. Tighten to 40—60 inch-pounds.
11. Install field brushes in insulated holders and position properly.
12. Place insulating washers on each brush terminal and install lockwashers and attaching screws. Be sure that brushes are not grounded.
13. Rotate pulley slowly by hand to make sure that fan blades do not hit stator windings.
14. Check alternator output after installing on car.

CHAPTER 8

Ford Alternators and Regulators

REAR TERMINAL ALTERNATOR

Description and Operation

The alternator produces power in the form of alternating current which is rectified to direct current by a system of six diodes (eight diodes in high-output alternators). The alternator regulator automatically adjusts the alternator field current to maintain the alternator output voltage within the prescribed limits to properly charge the battery. The alternator output is self-limiting. A Ford alternator charging system using an indicator lamp is shown in Fig. 8-1.

In systems using an indicator lamp, the circuit functions as follows: When the ignition switch is turned on, a small current flows through the lamp (turning it on) and through the regulator contacts to the alternator field coil. With the engine running, the rotating field produces a voltage in the stator windings. When the voltage at the alternator stator terminal reaches about 3 volts, the regulator field relay closes. This by-passes the indicator lamp (causing it to go out) and applies full system voltage to the regulator.

In ammeter-equipped systems (Fig. 8-2), the I terminal of the regulator and the stator terminal of the alternator are not used. (Note: The stator terminal may be used for an electric choke heater.) The field relay is closed by turning on the ignition switch. Initial field current for the alternator passes from the battery through the regulator terminal A to the alternator field coil. The method of energizing the field relay is the basic difference between the indicator-lamp system and the ammeter system. Once the alternator is turning, the two systems operate in the same manner. The am-

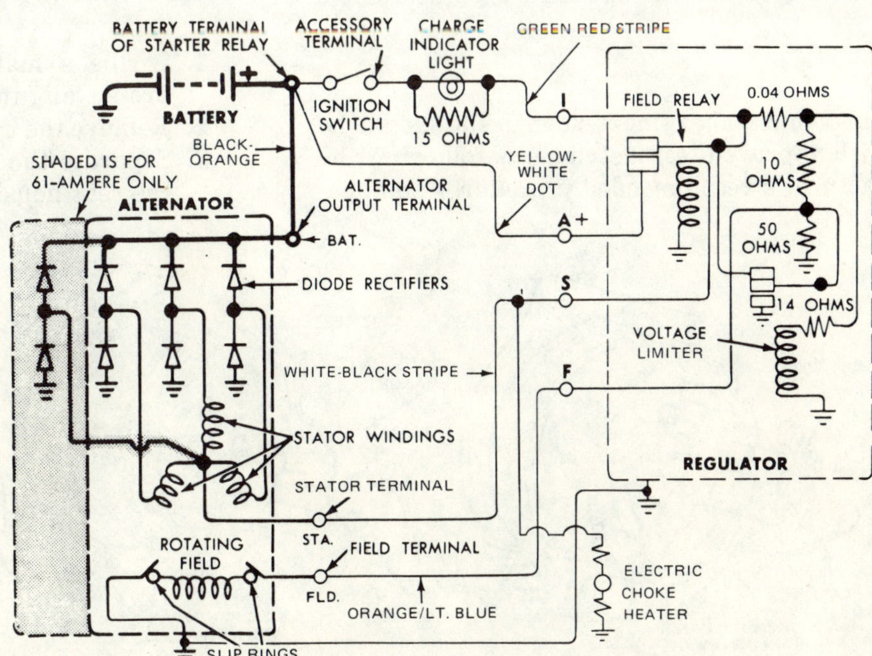

Fig. 8-1. Basic Ford alternator charging system with an indicator lamp.

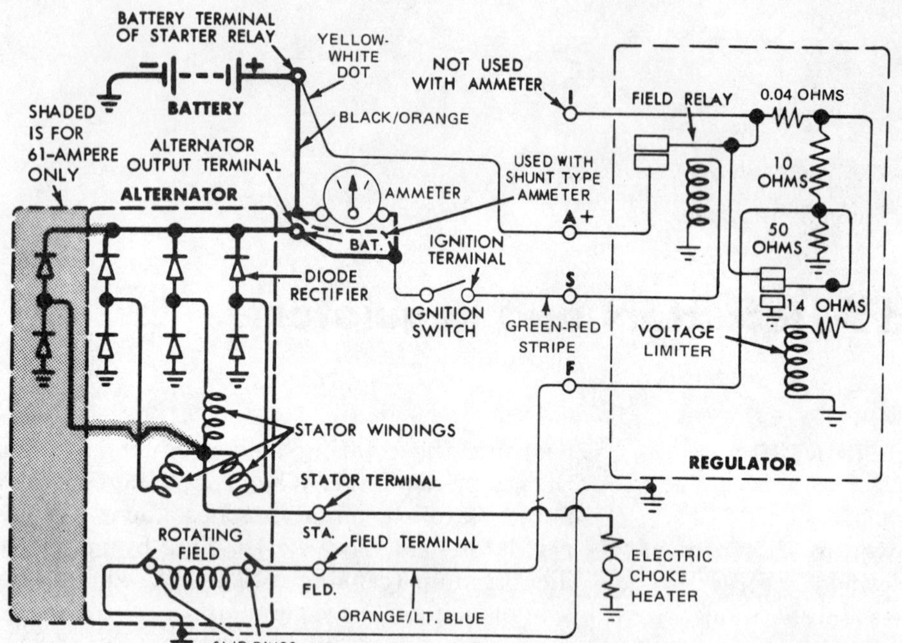

Fig. 8-2. Basic Ford alternator charging system equipped with an ammeter.

meter, though, shows the amount of current being delivered (charge) or drawn (discharge) from the battery.

Fusible links are included in the charging system to prevent damage to the wiring harness in the case of shorts or improper use of booster batteries. A fusible link is a short length of specially selected undersized wire that will burn open at a given current level. A vehicle may have one or more such fusible links. When a replacement is necessary, be sure to use the specified type of fusible link.

Testing

On-the-vehicle charging-system tests should be done with approved test instruments following the manufacturer's recommended procedures and specifications. Before testing, be sure that the alternator drive belt is tightened to the specified tension as measured with a belt-tension gauge.

When it is necessary to remove the alternator, be sure to disconnect the battery ground cable first. Leave the ground cable off until after the alternator has been completely reinstalled and all leads properly connected. See Fig. 8-3.

Disassembly and Overhaul

Fig. 8-4 shows a disassembled view of the alternator.

1. Scribe a mark on both end housings for proper alignment during reassembly.
2. Remove the three thru-bolts.
3. Separate the front housing and rotor from the rear housing and stator assembly.

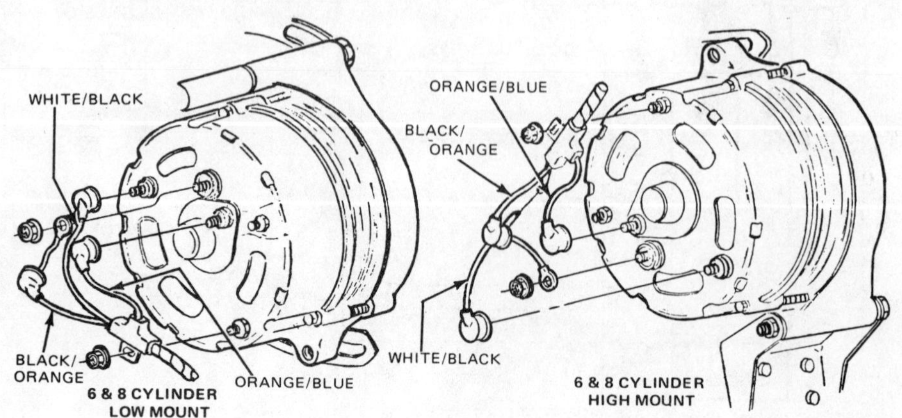

Fig. 8-3. Typical wiring harness connections.

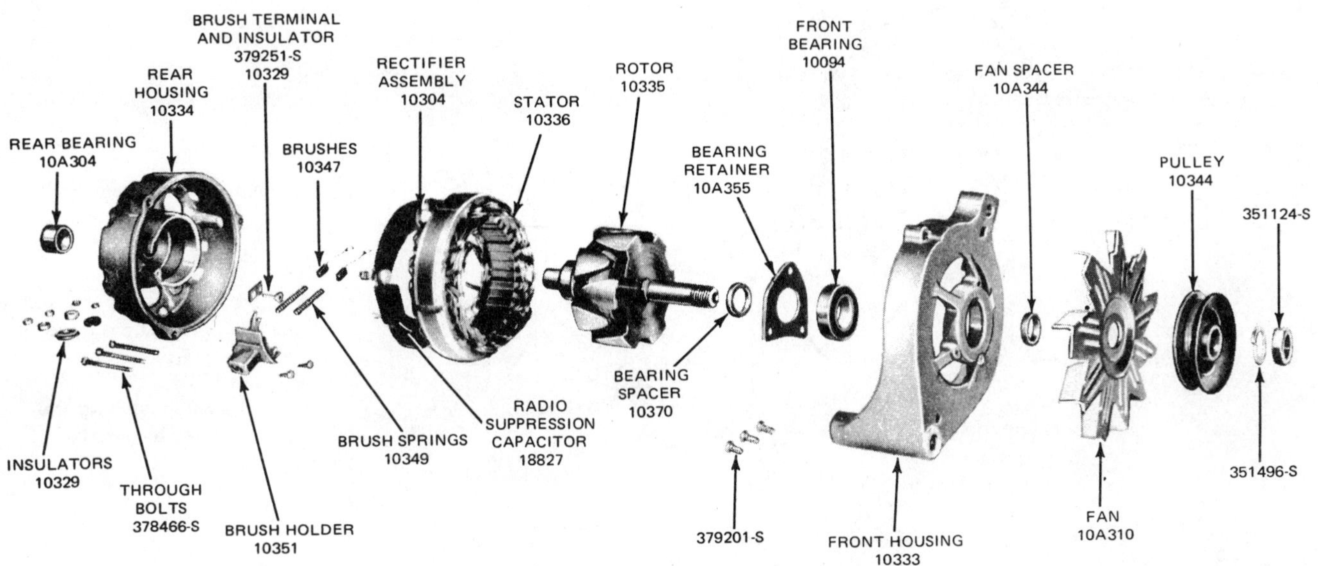

Fig. 8-4. Exploded view of disassembled alternator.

4. Remove all nuts and insulators from the rear housing and remove it from the stator and rectifier assembly.
5. Remove the brush-holder mounting screws and remove the brush holder, brushes, brush springs, insulator, and terminal.
6. If necessary, press the bearing from the rear housing. Support the housing on the inner boss when pressing out the bearing.
7. If the rectifier assembly is to be replaced, unsolder the stator leads from the printed-circuit board terminals and separate the stator from the rectifier assembly. Use a 100-watt iron.
8. Three types of rectifier-assembly circuit boards are used in the alternators. See Fig. 8-5. One type has the board spaced away from the diode plates with the diodes exposed; another type is a single circuit board with built-in diodes; the third type of rectifier assembly has built-in diodes with an additional booster-diode plate containing two diodes and is used only on high-output units.

If the rectifier assembly has an exposed circuit board, remove the screws from the assembly by rotating the bolt heads ¼ turn clockwise to unlock them. See Fig. 8-5. Push the stator terminal screw straight out on a rectifier assembly with the diodes built into

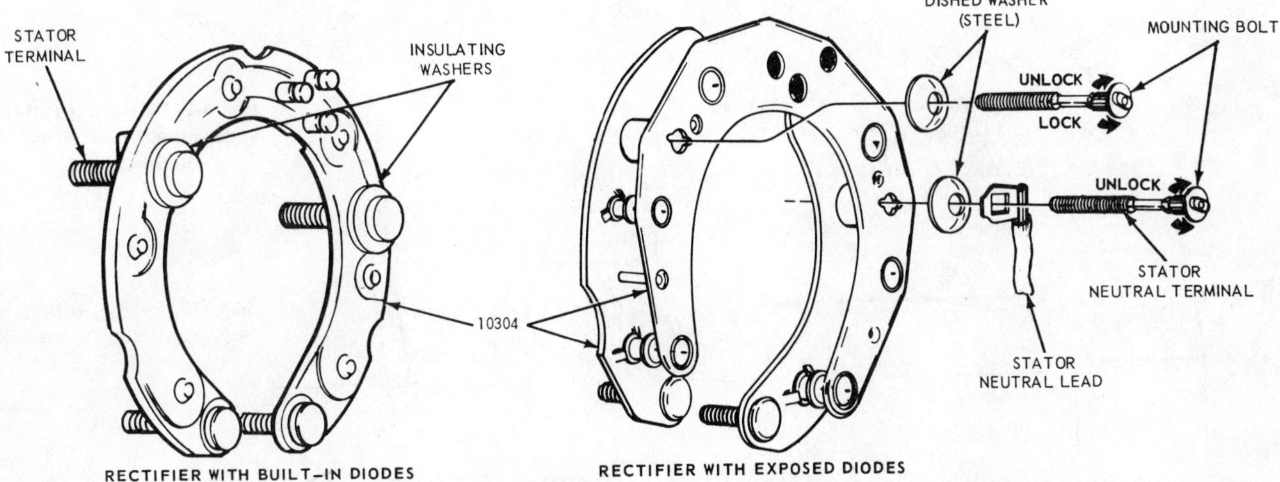

Fig. 8-5. Two types of rectifier assemblies.

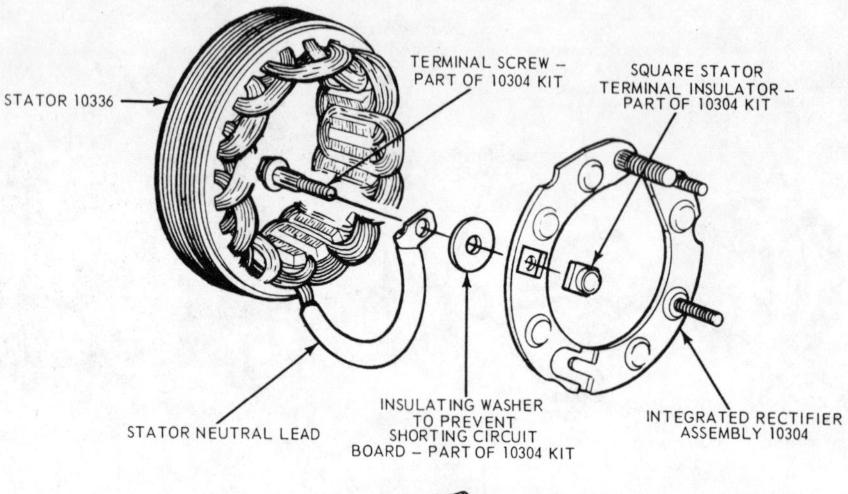

Fig. 8-6. Installing the stator terminals.

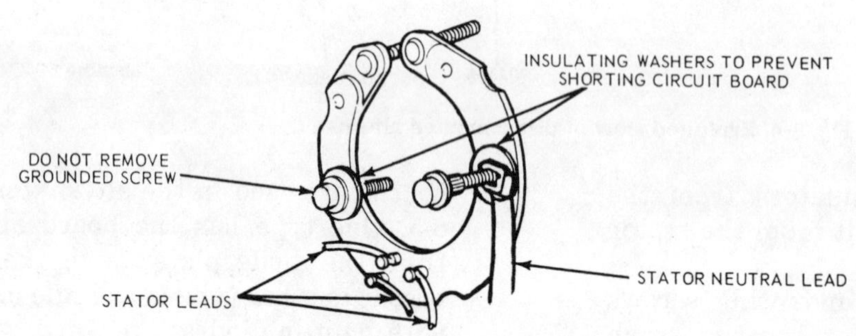

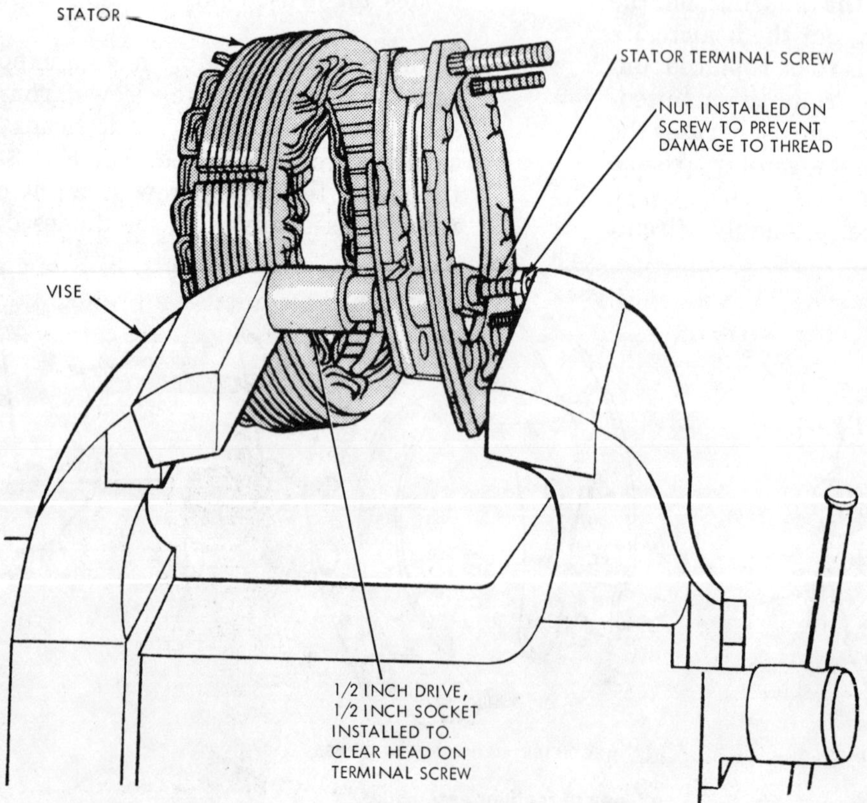

Fig. 8-7. Removing stator terminal screw from circuit board.

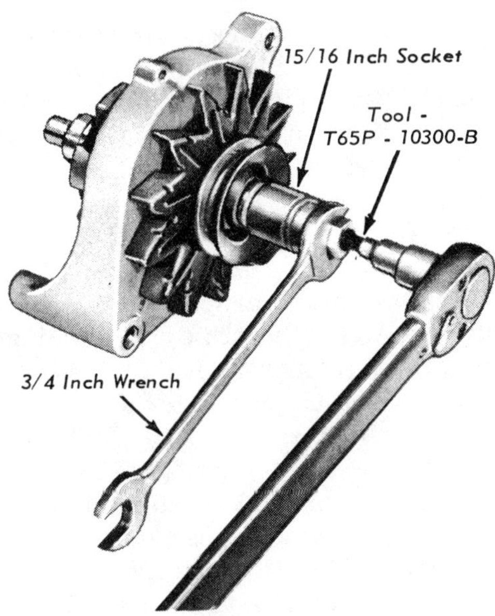

Fig. 8-8. Removing the pulley.

the circuit board. Avoid turning the screw while removing it to make certain that the straight knurl will engage the insulators when reinstalling the screw. Do not remove the grounded screw (Fig. 8-6). On high-output alternators, press the stator terminal screw from the circuit board as shown in Fig. 8-7. When the terminal screw has moved about ¼ inch, remove the nut and lift the screw from the board. Do not twist the screw in the board.

9. Remove the drive-pulley nut with the special tool shown in Fig. 8-8. Then pull the lockwasher, pulley, fan, fan spacer, front housing, and rotor stop from the rotor shaft.
10. Remove the three screws holding the front end retainer and remove the retainer. If necessary, press out the old bearing for replacement or lubrication.
11. Check the diodes and field coil with appropriate test instruments.

Assembly

1. Do not clean rotor, stator, or bearings with solvent. Wipe with a clean cloth.
2. Press the front bearing into the front bearing-housing boss, using pressure on the outer race only. Install the bearing retainer (see Fig. 8-4).
3. If stop ring on rotor shaft was damaged, install new ring. Push new ring on the shaft

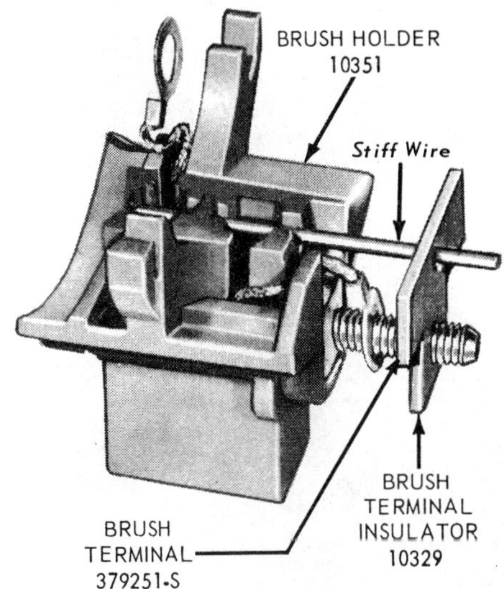

Fig. 8-9. Typical brush-holder assembly.

and into the groove. Do not attempt to open ring with snap-ring pliers as damage will result.
4. Position the rotor stop on the drive shaft with the recessed side against the stop ring.
5. Position the front housing, fan spacer, fan, pulley, and lockwasher on the drive shaft and install the retaining nut. Tighten nut with proper tool to the specified torque.
6. If replacing the rear bearing, support the housing on the inner boss and press in new bearing flush with the outer end surface.
7. Assemble the parts for the brush holder assembly and hold in place with a stiff wire as shown in Fig. 8-9.
8. Fasten the brush holder into the rear housing. See Fig. 8-10 for brush lead positioning.
9. Wrap the three stator leads around the circuit board terminals and solder them, using a 100-watt iron and rosin-core solder. Place the eyelet for the stator neutral lead eyelet

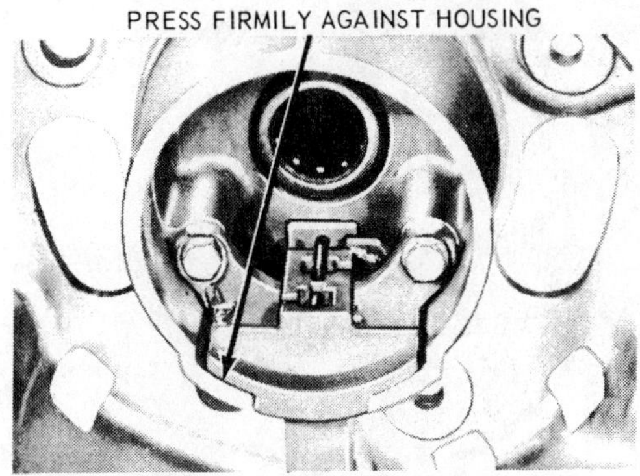

Fig. 8-10. Brush lead positions.

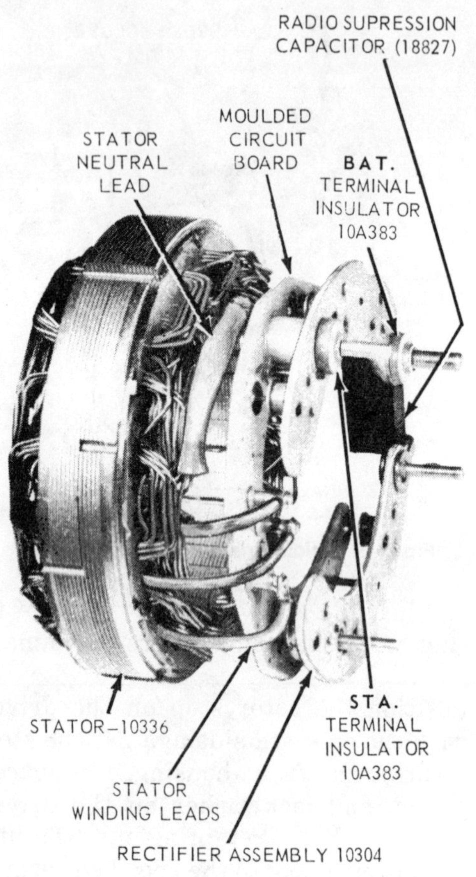

Fig. 8-11. Stator lead connections.

on the stator terminal screw and install the screw in the rectifier assembly. See Fig. 8-11.

10. For an exposed-diode rectifier assembly, insert the special screws through the wire lug, dished washers, and circuit board (see Fig. 8-5). Turn the screws ¼ turn counterclockwise to lock them. For single circuit boards with built-in diodes, insert the screws straight through the wire lug, the insulating washer, the square hole in the rectifier assembly, and into the insulator (Fig. 6-8). The dished washers are used only on the circuit boards with exposed diodes (Fig. 5-8). If they are used on the rectifier assembly with built-in diodes, a short circuit will occur. A flat insulating washer is to be used between the stator terminal and the integrated rectifier assembly.
11. For rectifiers with booster diode plate, proceed as follows:

    a. Place stator wire terminal on stator terminal screw and position screw into the rectifier. Position the insulator over the screw and into the square hole in the rectifier (Fig. 8-12).
    b. Rotate the terminal screw until it locks in position. Then press the screw in finger tight.
    c. Position the stator wire as shown in Fig. 8-13. Then press the terminal screw into the rectifier and insulator as shown in Fig. 8-14.

12. Position the suppression capacitor on the rectifier terminals. On the board with exposed diodes, install the STA and BAT terminal insulators (Fig. 8-11). On the single circuit board, position the square stator terminal insulator in the square hole in the rectifier assembly (Fig. 8-6). Position the BAT terminal insulator as shown in Fig. 8-15.

Position the stator-rectifier assembly in the

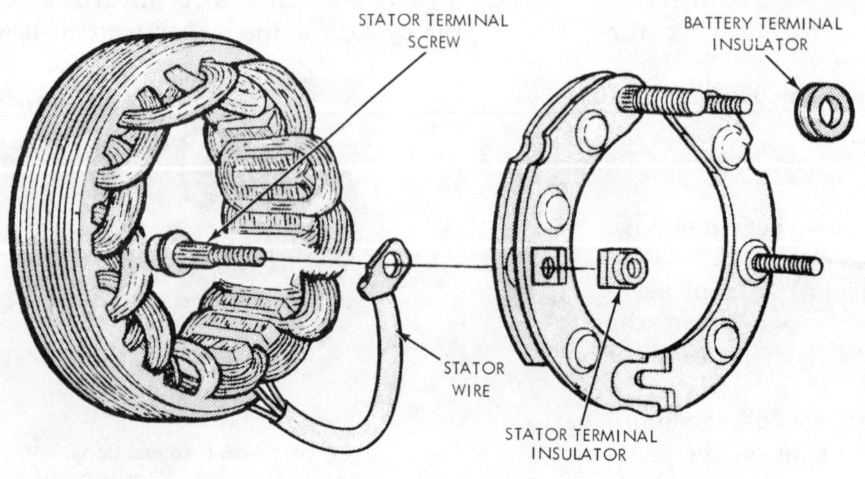

Fig. 8-12. Stator and rectifier assembly for 61-ampere alternator.

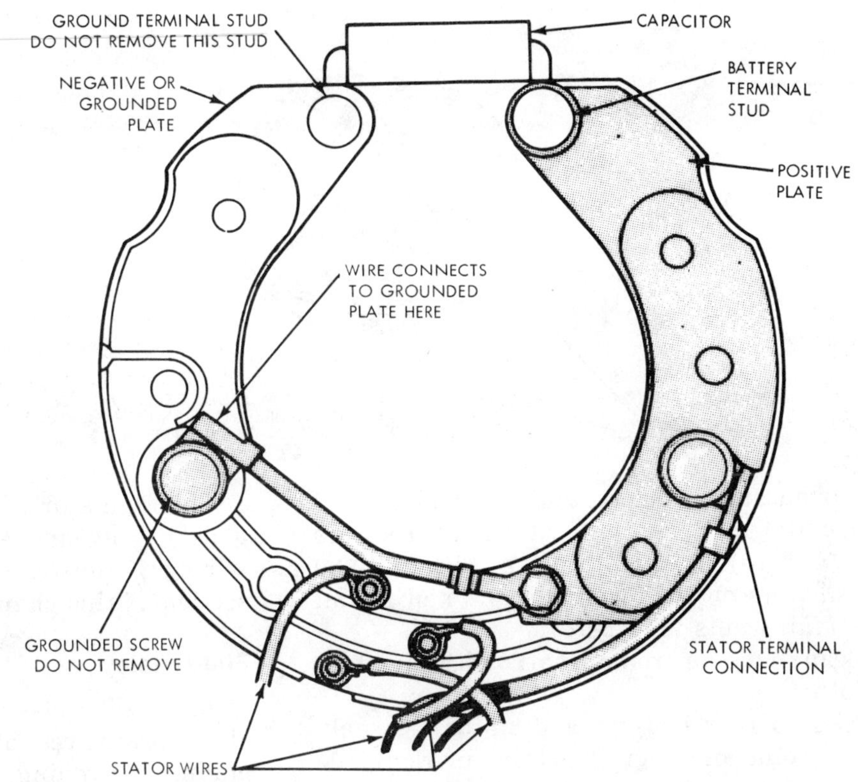

Fig. 8-13. Location of rectifier terminals on 61-ampere alternator.

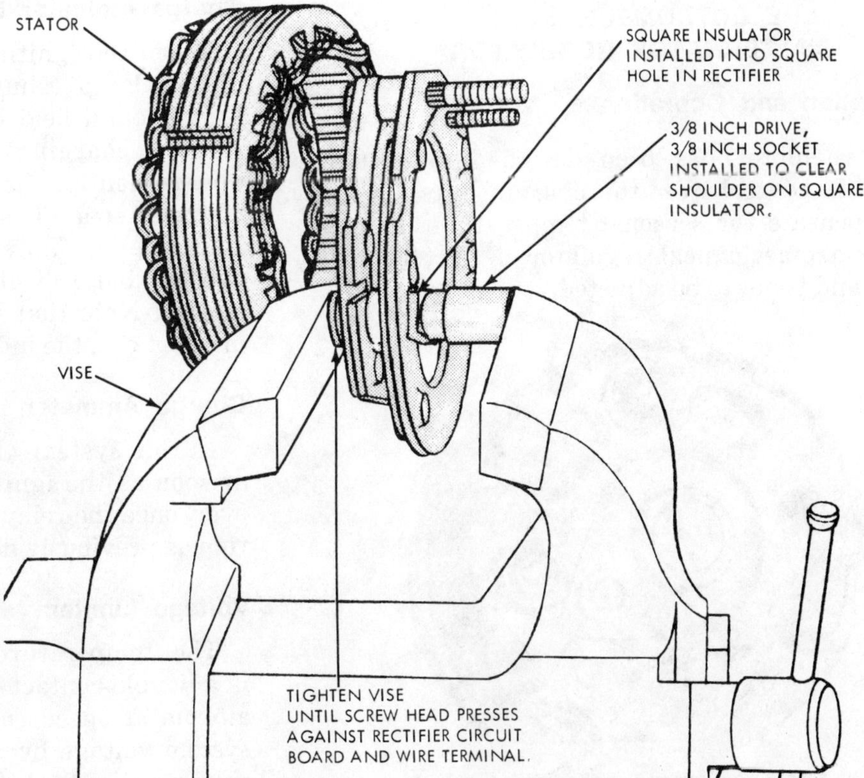

Fig. 8-14. Installation of stator terminal on 61-ampere alternator.

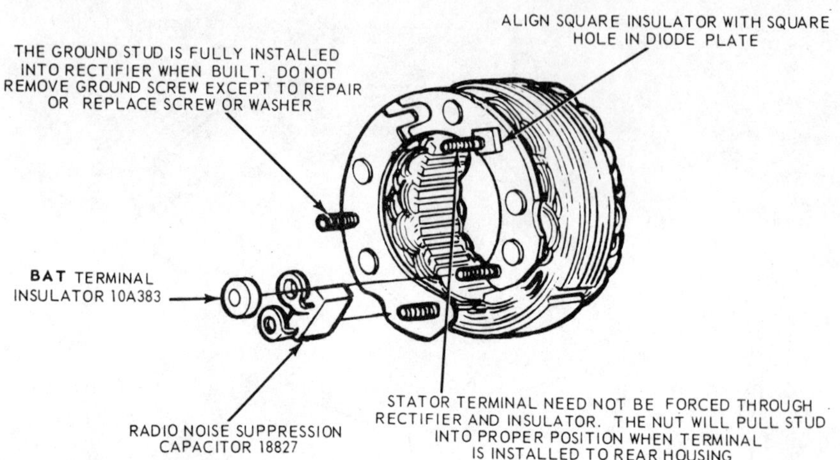

Fig. 8-15. Installing the terminal insulator on the single circuit board.

rear housing, Make certain that all terminal insulators are properly seated in the recesses (Fig. 8-15). Position the STA, BAT, and FLD insulators on the terminal bolts and install retaining nuts (Fig. 8-16).

13. Clean ends of rotor shaft with lint-free cloth.
14. Position rear housing and stator assembly over rotor and align the scribe marks made during disassembly. After attaching thru-bolts, remove brush retracting wire.

ELECTROMECHANICAL ALTERNATOR REGULATOR

Description and Operation

The regulator has been designed to exercise automatic control over the charging system and to compensate for seasonal temperature changes. The electromechanical regulator is factory calibrated and is not to be adjusted.

Fig. 8-16. Locations of the alternator terminals.

The regulator is composed of two control units, a field relay and a voltage limiter. The internal wiring is illustrated in Figs. 8-1 and 8-2 in the section of this chapter covering the alternator.

Field Relay

The field relay connects the alternator field circuit to the rest of the charging circuit when the engine is running. The circuit that controls this relay varies according to whether the system utilizes an ammeter or an indicator lamp.

Charge Indicator Lamp

When the ignition switch closes, the charge indicator lamp (shunted by a 15-ohm resistor) allows enough field current to flow to start the alternator charging. When alternator voltage builds up sufficiently, the voltage at the stator terminal of the alternator is enough to close the field relay. This applies full system voltage to the field circuit so that full alternator output is available if needed. Note that the field-relay contacts bypass, or short out, the indicator lamp.

Charge Ammeter

In this system (Fig. 8-2), the field relay closes as soon as the ignition switch is turned on. However, once the relay closes, it serves the same function as previously described.

Voltage Limiter

The temperature-compensated voltage limiter is a double-contact type for effective control at all alternator speeds and electrical loads. It controls system voltage by controlling the amount of current supplied to the field coils.

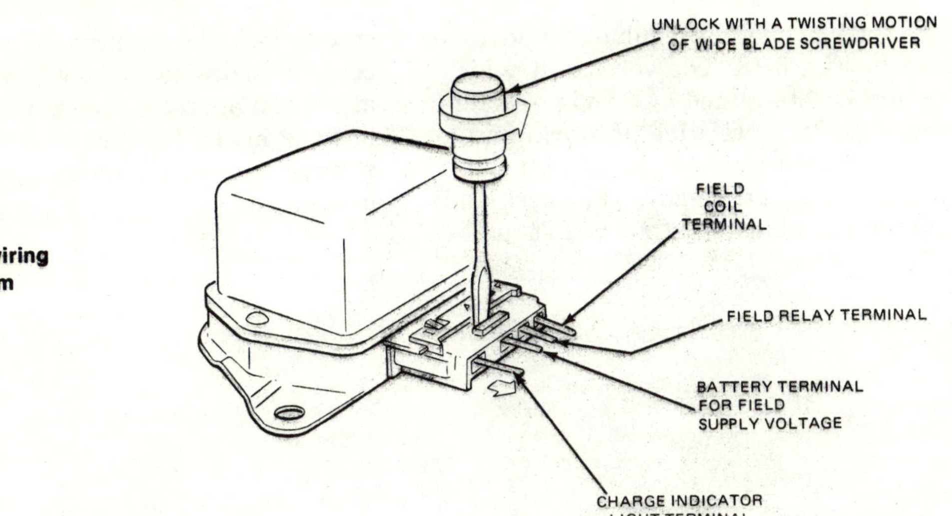

Fig. 8-17. Unlocking the wiring harness connector from the regulator.

Testing

Use an approved type of charging-system tester and follow the manufacturer's recommended test procedures. Be sure that the drive belt is properly tightened. A general testing procedure is given below.

1. Connect positive voltmeter lead to the positive battery post and the negative voltmeter lead to ground. Note the voltage reading.
2. Turn off all electrical accessories.
3. Operate engine at 1800—2200 rpm for 2 to 3 minutes.
4. At this speed, note the voltmeter reading. It should be 1 to 2 volts higher than the voltage observed in step 1. This is the regulated voltage.
5. If the voltage difference is less than 1 volt or greater than 2½ volts, replace the regulator.
6. If the voltage is within the prescribed limits, turn on the headlights and blower motor. The voltage should not drop more than a half volt from the regulated voltage. If it drops more than this, replace the regulator.

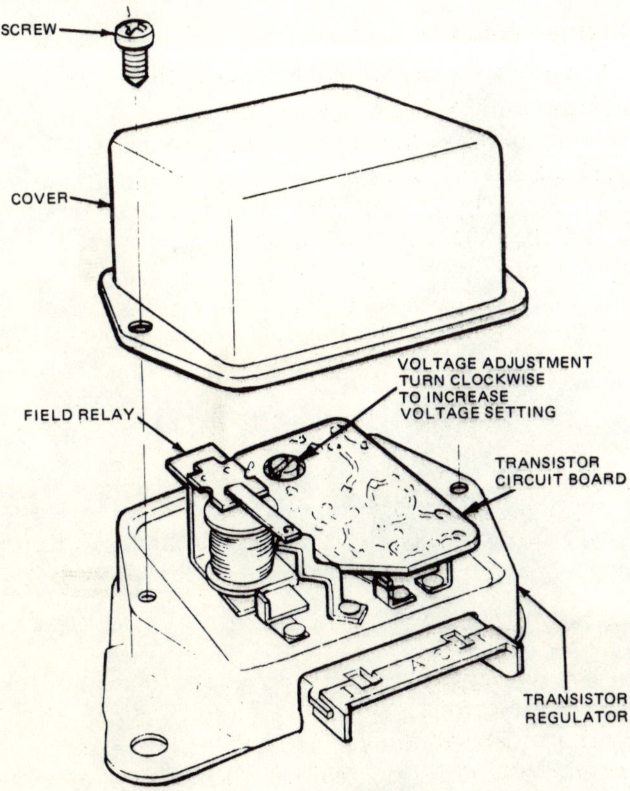

Fig. 8-18. The Ford transistorized regulator.

NOTE: The regulator is factory calibrated and sealed, and no attempt should be made to adjust it. If the regulator does not operate as specified, it must be replaced. Fig. 8-17 shows how to unlock terminal strip to replace the regulator.

TRANSISTORIZED REGULATOR

Description and Operation

The transistorized voltage regulator (Fig. 8-18) controls the alternator voltage output in a manner similar to an electromechanical regulator by regulating the alternator field current. The regulation is accomplished electronically with the use of transistors and diodes rather than by a vibrating relay armature.

The voltage setting for this regulator is adjustable as shown in Fig. 8-18. The voltage at which regulation occurs is determined by a voltage-reference (or zener) diode, a resistive network, and a transistor.

To adjust this regulator, remove the cover and use a fiber rod to the adjustment screw. Turn the screw clockwise to increase the voltage setting and counterclockwise to decrease it. The unit must be at normal operating temperature when the adjustment is made. Be sure to use an accurate test instrument to monitor regulated voltage during this procedure.

CHAPTER 9

Servicing American Motors Charging Systems

This chapter provides on-vehicle testing procedures for two basic styles of alternators manufactured by Motorola. The current-output ratings (marked on the units) are: 35, 37, 55, and 62 amperes, depending on the particular model. All of these alternators are designed for 12-volt systems with negative ground.

The unit shown in Fig. 9-1 has an ac output terminal; the unit shown in Fig. 9-2 does not have an ac terminal. Essentially, the two styles are similar as far as testing and servicing are concerned. What other differences there are will be covered in the following procedures.

TEST NO. 1—OPEN FIELD DIODE TEST

Test conditions: Ignition on, engine running (see Fig. 9-3). This test determines if the battery is properly connected to the alternator. It also determines if the field diode assembly has an open condition. It should be remembered that an improperly connected battery can damage not only the alternator, but the regulator as well.

The field diode assembly consists of three separate diodes mounted to a heat sink that makes a common connection at the regulator terminal of the alternator. If all three field diodes are open, alternator operation would cease, resulting in the eventual discharge of the battery. However, should only one or two field diodes open, battery charging action would still continue, but at a lower rate.

Referring to Fig. 9-3, connect the negative voltmeter lead to ground and the positive lead to the alternator output terminal. The voltmeter will indicate battery voltage. With the voltmeter still connected, check the leads between the alternator

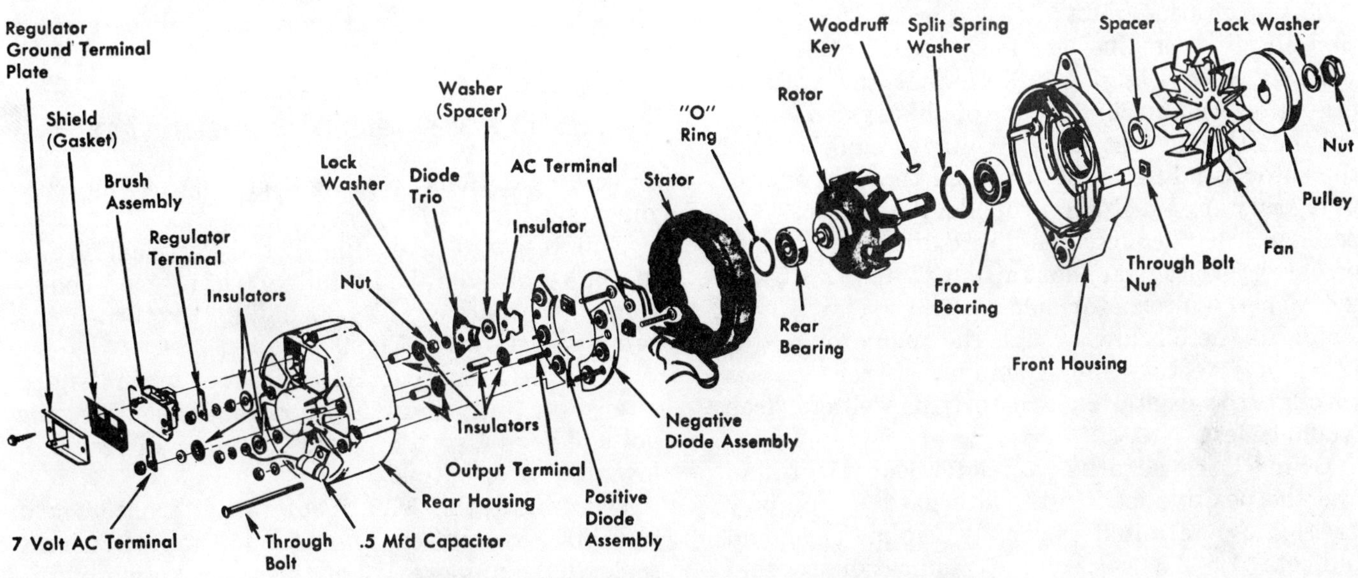

Fig. 9-1. Exploded view of the alternator with an ac terminal.

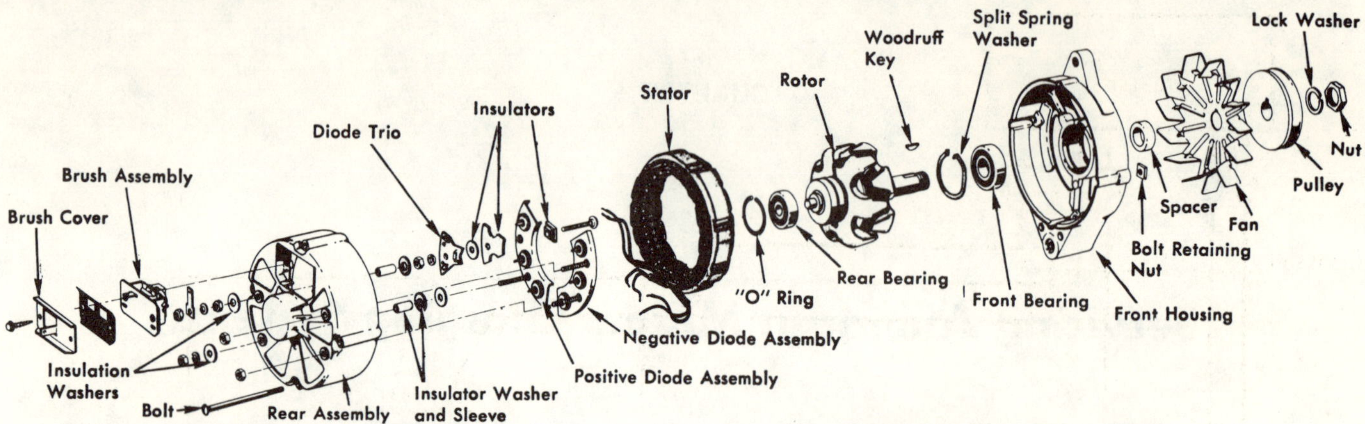

Fig. 9-2. Exploded view of the alternator without an ac terminal.

and the battery by moving them. If this causes the voltmeter reading to vary, loose connections are indicated. Repair as needed.

Move the positive voltmeter lead to the regulator terminal of the alternator. The voltmeter reading at this point should be approximately the same as at the output terminal. A lower-than-normal reading may be an indication that one or more field diodes are open. The alternator must be removed for field diode replacement.

TEST NO. 2—EXCITATION-VOLTAGE AND POSITIVE-RECTIFIER TESTS

Test conditions: (A) Excitation-voltage test—Ignition on, engine not running. (B) Positive rectifier diode test—Ignition off, engine not running (see Figs. 9-4 and 9-5).

The excitation-voltage test checks the excitation circuit from the ignition switch to the rotor winding (see Fig. 9-5). Note that the voltage-regulator load circuit is part of this system.

When the current for the voltage regulator and the rotor winding passes through the field excitation resistor, a voltage drop develops across the resistor. This reduces the approximately 12 volts of battery voltage at the ignition switch to 1.5–2.5 volts on the alternator side of field excitation resistor. If the circuit through the regulator or the rotor is defective and a smaller current passes through the excitation resistor, the voltage drop would be less.

Connect the negative voltmeter lead to ground and the positive lead to the alternator's auxiliary (regulator) terminal. Normally, the meter should indicate 1.5–2.5 volts. Fault indications would typically be:

1. Open rotor circuit; 5.0–7.0 volts.
2. Grounded rotor circuit: 0.75–1.1 volts.
3. Open in regulator load circuit: 8.5–10.0 volts.
4. Open switch or excitation resistor: zero volts.

If the initial test results are inconclusive, the voltage regulator may be bypassed with a short jumper between the auxiliary (regulator) and the field terminals of the alternator. If the jumper provides approximately correct voltage, the fault is in the regulator. No change from a high voltage reading indicates that the defect is in the brush or rotor circuit. The rotor may be checked in more detail as outlined in Test No. 4.

The positive-rectifier diode test is made by connecting test equipment to the alternator as shown in Fig. 9-4. Zero voltage is the correct voltmeter reading. If a higher voltage reading is obtained, the alternator must be removed and disassembled for repair.

TEST NO. 3—FIELD CURRENT TEST

Test conditions: Ignition off, engine not running (see Fig. 9-6).

This test will determine if the electrical circuit of the rotor (the field winding) is in good condition. The field circuit, including the brush assembly, is shown in Fig. 9-7.

High field current may produce uncontrolled alternator output and probable damage to the voltage regulator. Low field current will result in low alternator output.

Disconnect the lead from the alternator field terminal. Switch test ammeter to the low current scale (0–10 amperes). Set the control knob of the field rheostat to the maximum-resistance position.

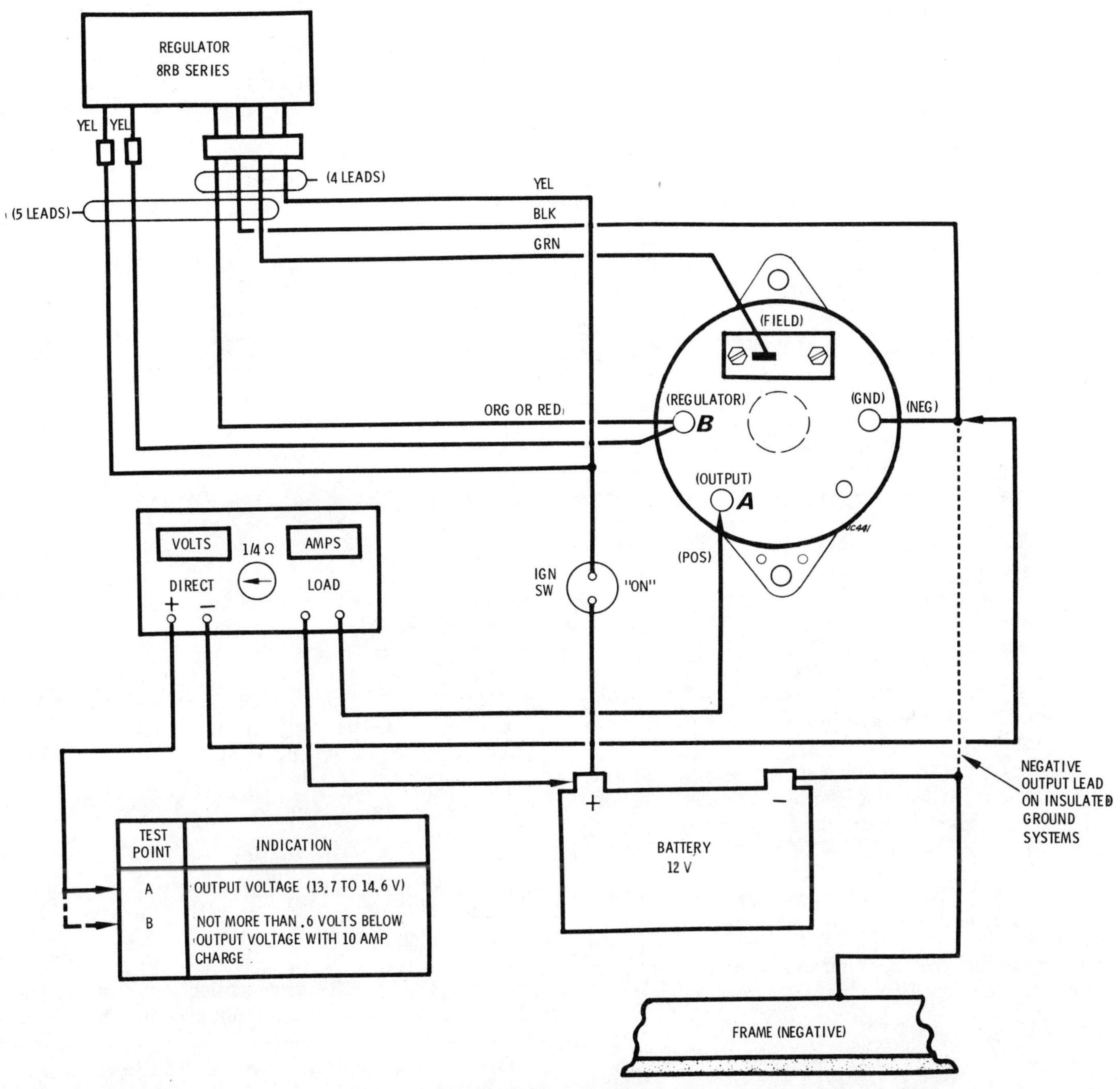

TEST POINT	INDICATION
A	OUTPUT VOLTAGE (13.7 TO 14.6 V)
B	NOT MORE THAN .6 VOLTS BELOW OUTPUT VOLTAGE WITH 10 AMP CHARGE

Fig. 9-3. Test connections to check for open field diodes.

The field rheostat will prevent damage to the test ammeter if the rotor winding is shorted or grounded. Connect the field rheostat and the test ammeter in series between the alternator output terminal and the field terminals as shown in Fig. 9-6.

Slowly reduce the resistance of the field rheostat while noting the test ammeter reading. If the resistance of the field rheostat can be reduced to zero with the ammeter indicating less than 3.5 amperes, the field winding is neither shorted nor grounded. The test ammeter reading with no rheostat resistance is the current drawn by the rotor (or field winding).

Typically, this is about 2.0 to 2.5 amperes at a nominal battery voltage of 12.0–12.6 volts. If the

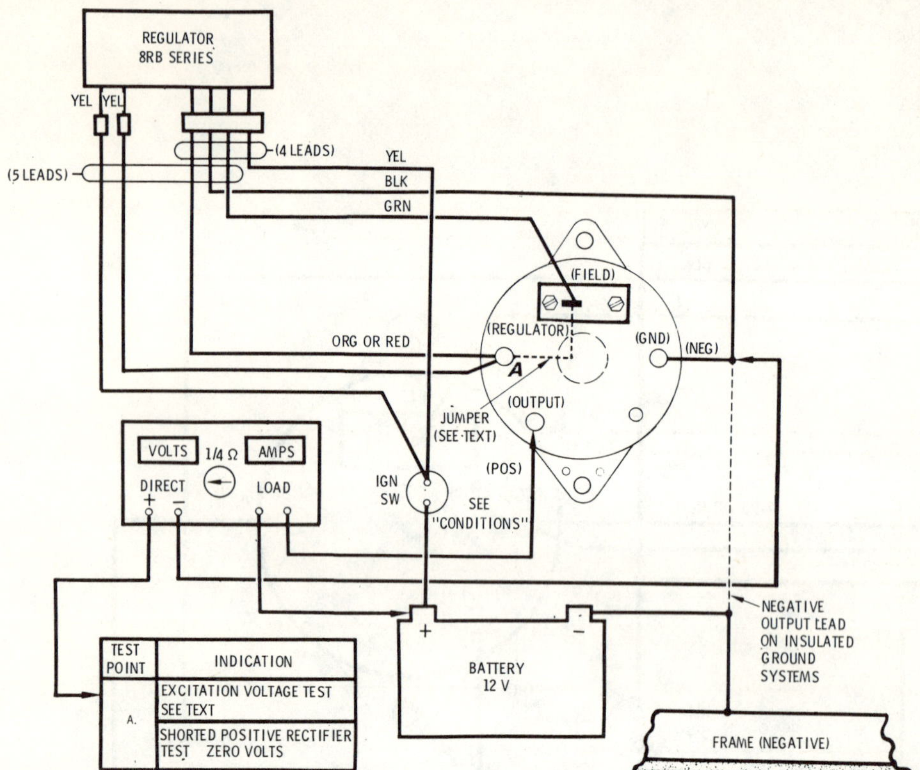

Fig. 9-4. Test connections for the excitation-voltage test.

ammeter reading tends to vary when the rotor is turned slightly, the slip rings and brushes should be cleaned. Use a fine grade of crocus cloth for this purpose.

If normal rotor current cannot be obtained, the alternator must be disassembled for replacement of defective parts. If the field current is normal, proceed to the next test.

TEST NO. 4—REGULATOR OPERATING VOLTAGE TEST

Test conditions: Ignition on, engine running at fast idle (see Fig. 9-8).

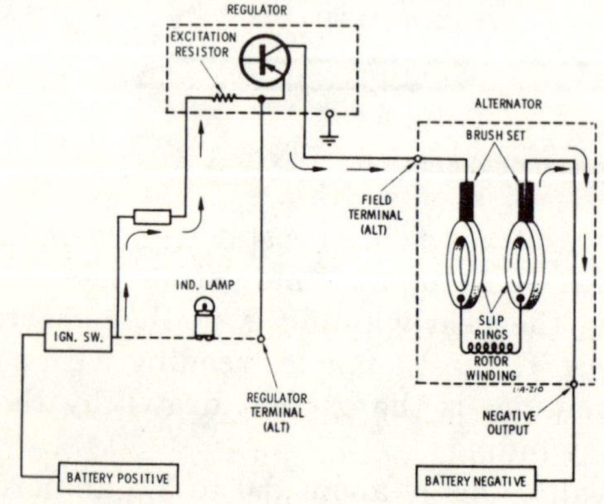

Fig. 9-5. The excitation cicruit.

This test determines the operating level of the voltage regulator. Such voltage tests are most accurate when the battery is fully charged since the alternator current output is at a minimum at this time. Under this condition, the charging voltage will rise to the maximum level allowed by the regulator.

A ¼-ohm, 25-watt resistor may be placed in series with the alternator output leads to reduce charging current to about 8–10 amperes. This simulates the charging rate of a nearly fully charged battery even though the battery is at less than full charge. The test connections for the ¼-ohm resistor and test ammeter are shown in Fig. 9-8.

Connect the positive voltmeter lead to the alternator's output terminal and the negative lead to ground. Run the engine for a few minutes to stabilize component temperatures. The voltage indicated by the meter is the level established by the regulator and is usually between 13.9 and 14.7 volts, depending on the ambient temperature of the regulator.

A high voltage indication may be due to a poor regulator ground connection. The regulator circuit is usually grounded through a separate lead which must make a clean and tight connection at

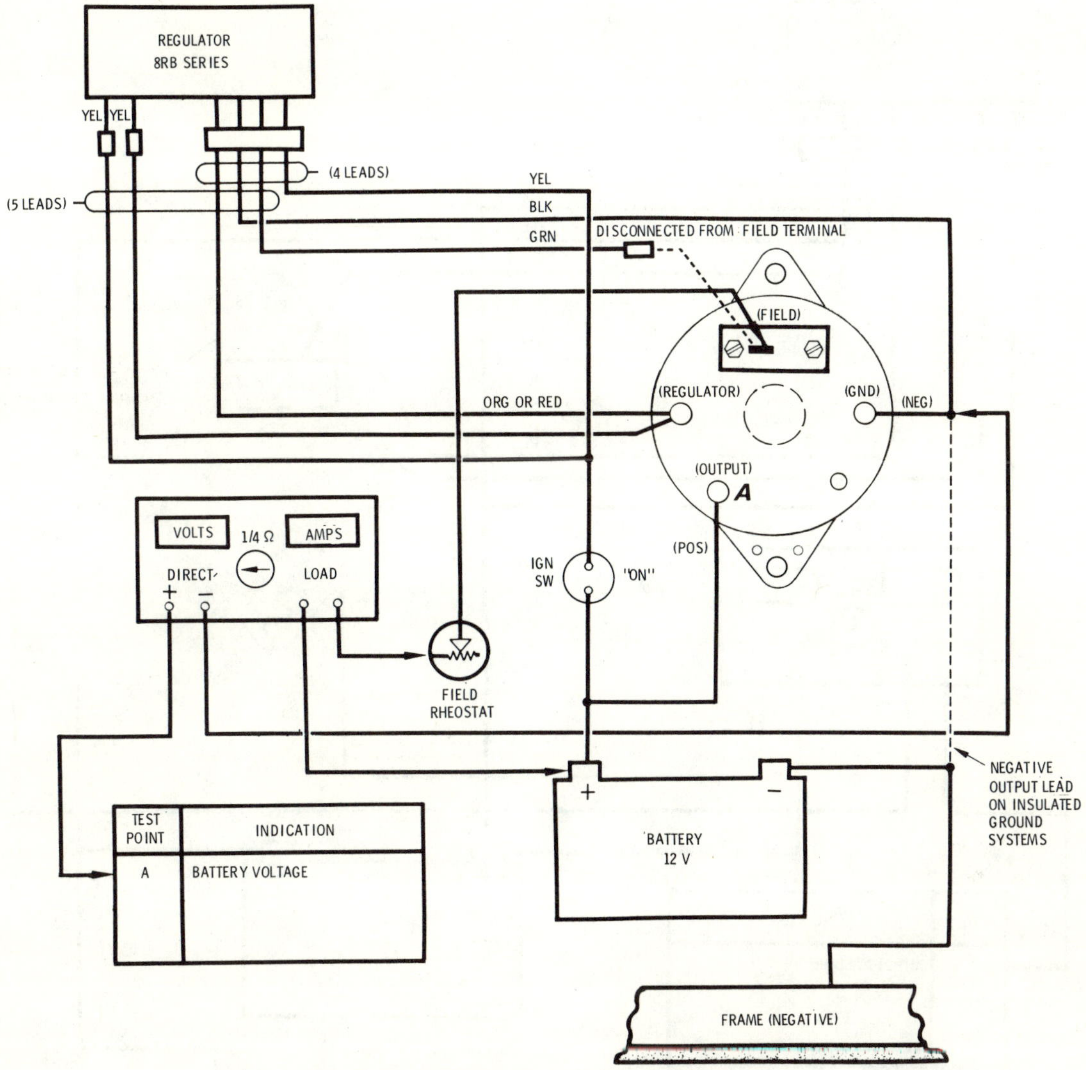

TEST POINT	INDICATION
A	BATTERY VOLTAGE

Fig. 9-6. Test connections for the field current test.

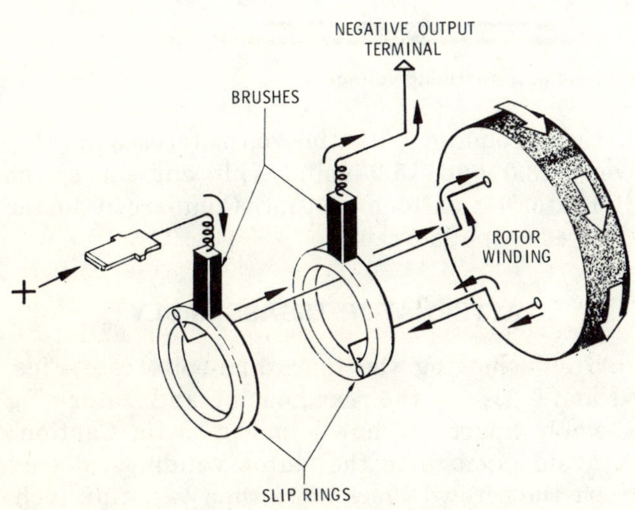

Fig. 9-7. Rotor winding test.

the alternator ground. If the high voltage is not caused by a faulty ground, the trouble probably lies within the regulator. If the defect is in the regulator, it must be replaced.

Be sure to remove the ¼-ohm resistor at the completion of this test.

TEST NO. 5—ALTERNATOR OUTPUT TEST

Test conditions: Ignition on, engine running (see Fig. 9-9).

This test checks the alternator's ability to produce its maximum output current. A carbon pile is connected across the battery to induce maximum charging current. Fig. 9-9 shows this connection.

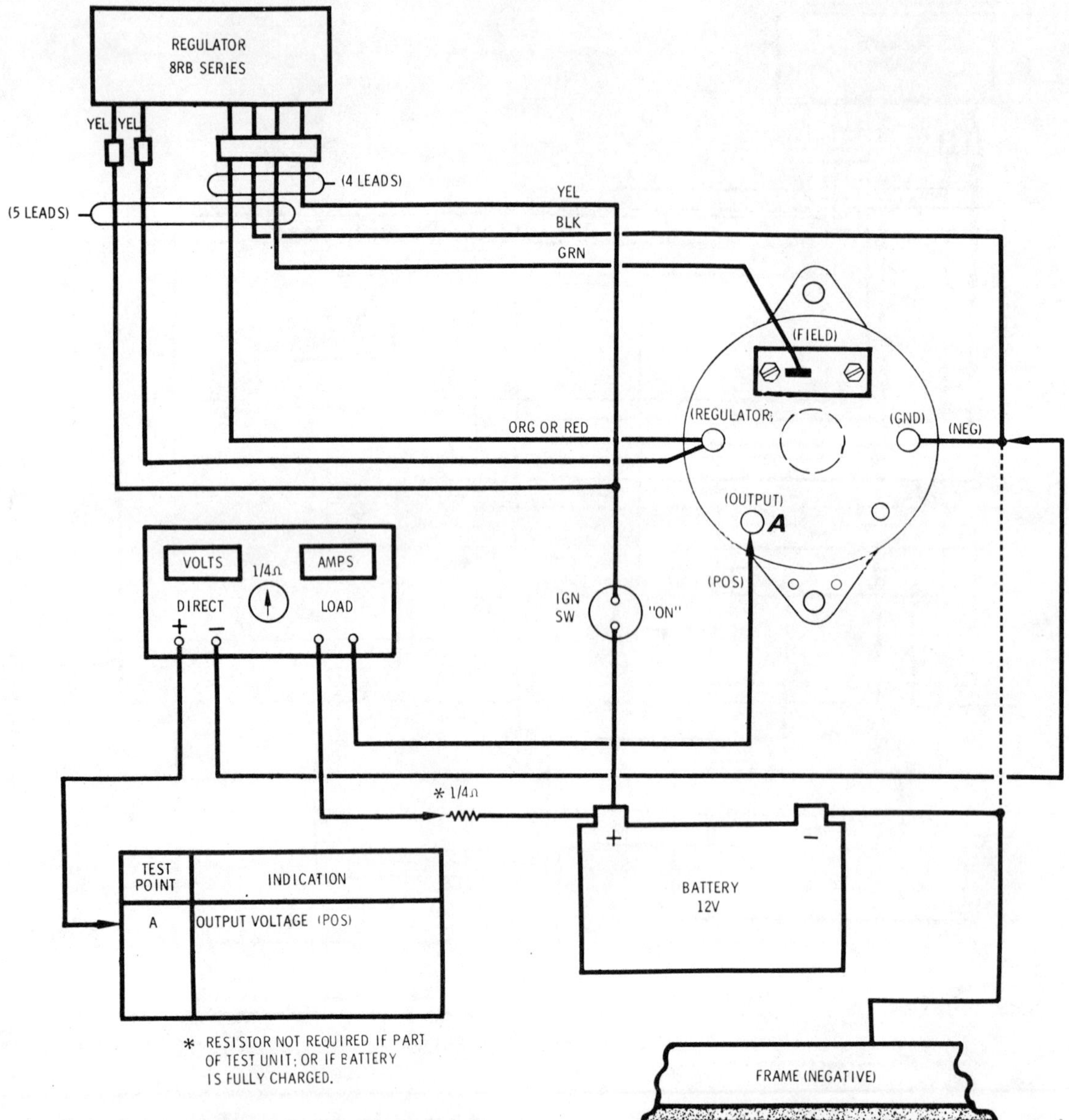

Fig. 9-8. Test connections for determining regulator operating voltage.

Place the ammeter in the 0–100-ampere (or greater) range. Unload the carbon pile before connecting it to the battery. Operate the engine at fast idle and apply the carbon-pile load (or vehicle accessory load) to produce a 20-ampere charge rate. Charge at this rate for a few minutes to warm up the components. A low charge rate is usually due to a faulty regulator. Replace the regulator if necessary.

Set engine speed so as to produce an alternator speed of approximately 3000–4000 rpm. (NOTE: Engine speed is less than alternator speed.) Increase the carbon-pile load, noting the maximum current produced with the voltmeter reading between 13.0 and 15.0 volts. This current is the alternator's maximum output. Compare it to the specified output current.

ALTERNATOR DISASSEMBLY

After removing the four thru-bolts (see Figs. 9-1 and 9-2), pry the rear housing and stator-ring assembly apart as shown in Fig. 9-10. Caution: To avoid damage to the stator windings, do not insert the screwdrivers more than 1/16 of an inch. The rotor will remain with the front housing.

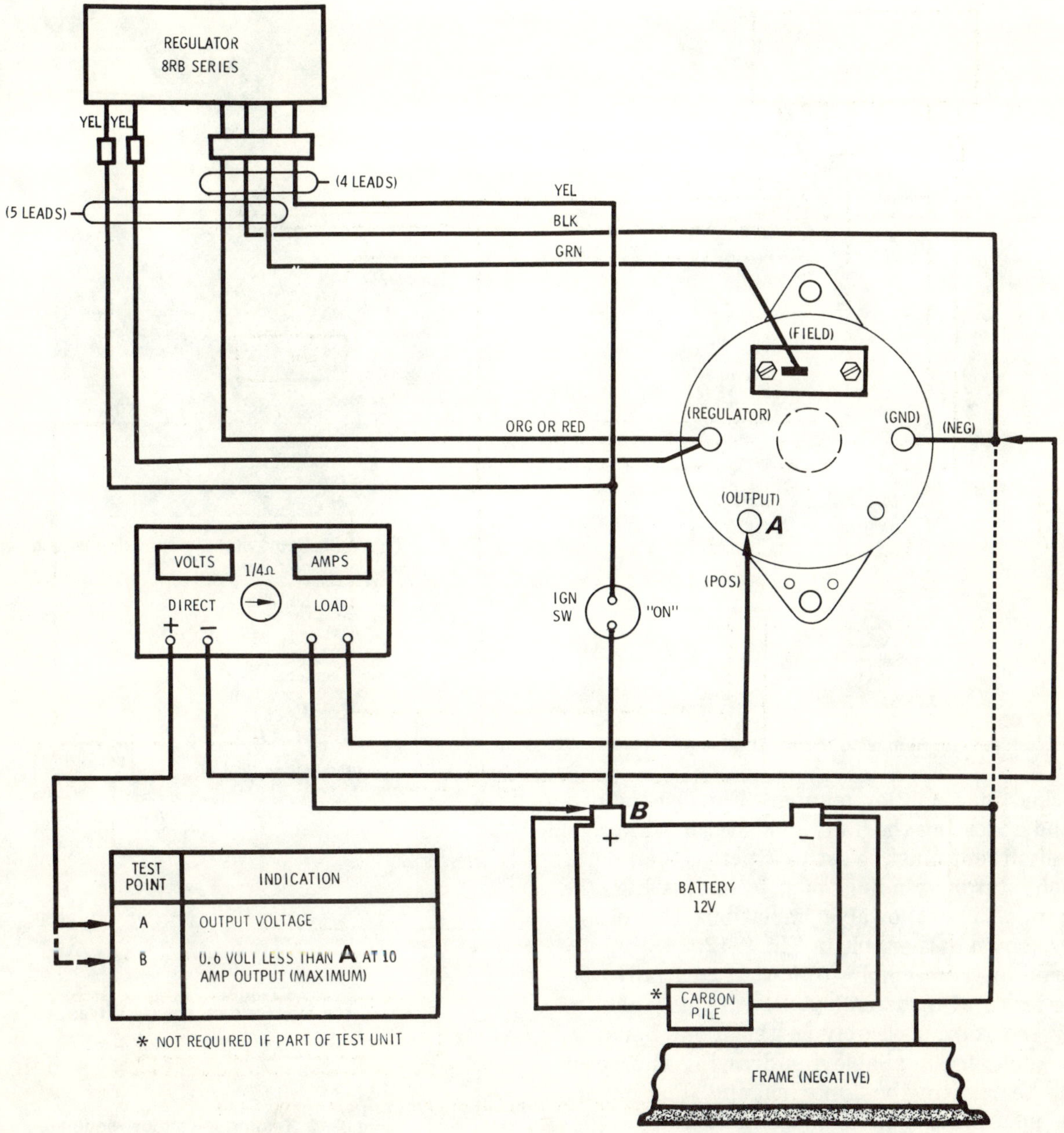

TEST POINT	INDICATION
A	OUTPUT VOLTAGE
B	0.6 VOLT LESS THAN **A** AT 10 AMP OUTPUT (MAXIMUM)

Fig. 9-9. Test connections for alternator output test.

Normally, it is not necessary to disassemble the rotor from the front housing unless there is damage to the rotor. The rotor winding can be checked for proper resistance (typically 5–7 ohms) with an ohmmeter or by the on-vehicle method described earlier in this chapter. Should rotor disassembly be necessary, remove the split-spring washer from behind the front bearing as shown in Fig. 9-11.

Before the rotor can be removed, the pulley must be removed from the rotor shaft. Use a double-jaw puller for this purpose. The front and rear bearings will be attached to the rotor assembly after it has been removed from the front housing. These bearings are permanently lubricated and sealed. Should they require replacement, they can be removed with a suitable bearing puller. When replacing the front bearing, it should be installed in the front housing first.

The diode assemblies can be tested with any of the standard test instruments used for other alternators. The field diode (or diode trio) can also

Fig. 9-10. Removing the rear housing.

be checked in a similar manner. Fig. 9-12 shows a method of testing the individual stator windings. The test current must be set to exactly 20 amperes for each stator winding test by adjusting the carbon pile. The allowable variations in voltage drops is shown in the table in Fig. 9-12.

Alternator reassembly follows essentially the reverse order of disassembly. Be careful when installing the rotor assembly in the front housing. Special tools are available for drawing the rotor into the bearing in the front housing. For proper parts sequence, refer to Figs. 9-1 and 9-2.

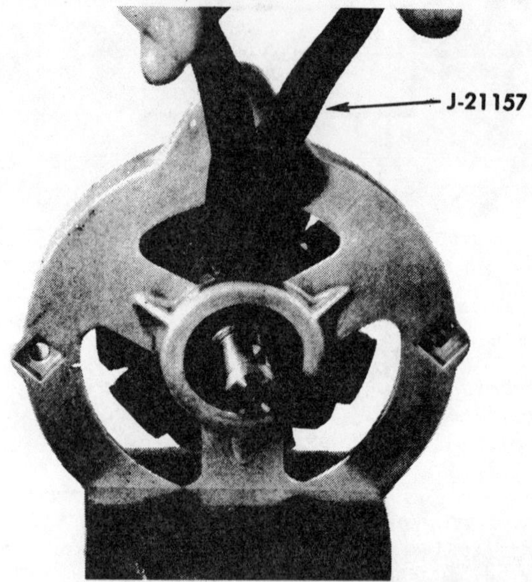

Fig. 9-11. Removing the split-ring washer.

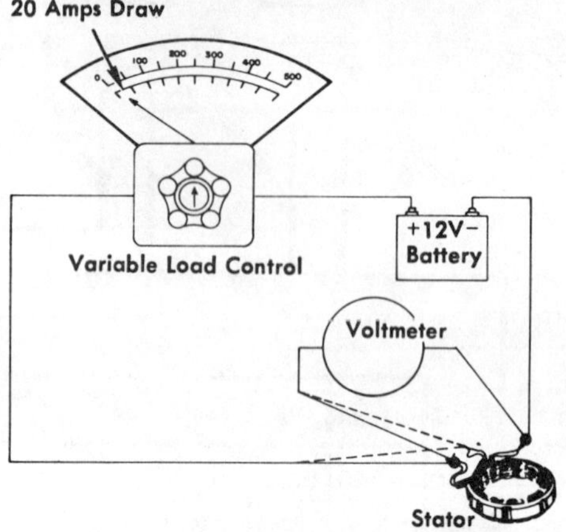

ALTERNATOR	MAXIMUM VOLTAGE DROP	MAXIMUM VARIANCE BETWEEN WINDINGS
37	4.2	.6
51	7.7	.4
62	5.0	.4

Fig. 9-12. Testing the stator windings.

Index